Sunset
Cookies
STEP-BY-STEP TECHNIQUES

By the Editors of Sunset Books
and Sunset Magazine

Lane Publishing Co. • Menlo Park, California

Cookies!

Freshly baked cookies are among the world's best-loved foods, enjoyed by young and old alike. Part of the joy of cookies is their versatility—in this book you'll find recipes for every occasion, from after-school snacking to elegant entertaining. In addition, our step-by-step photographs will acquaint you with some of the more unusual cookie-baking techniques, such as how to shape fortune cookies and how to build a gingerbread log cabin.

For their generosity in sharing props for use in our photographs, we're grateful to Best of All Worlds, Brass International, House of Today, S. Christian of Copenhagen, William Ober Co., and Williams-Sonoma Kitchenware. We extend special thanks to Diane Mancari for her culinary assistance with our photography, and to Rebecca La Brum for her thorough and thoughtful editing of the manuscript.

Research & Text
Claire Coleman

Coordinating Editor
Linda J. Selden

Special Consultant
Joan Griffiths

Design
Lea Damiano Phelps

Illustrations
Jacqueline Osborn

Photography
Darrow M. Watt

Photo Editor
Lynne B. Morrall

Cover: One of the simple pleasures of life is a glass of milk and a plate of homemade cookies. The hard-to-resist snack on our cover includes (clockwise from top right) Applesauce-Raisin Brownies (page 23), Raspberry-Nut Valentines (page 84), and—everybody's favorite—Chocolate Chip Cookies at Their Best (page 10). Photograph by Nikolay Zurek. Cover design by Lynne B. Morrall.

Sunset Books
  Editor, David E. Clark
  Managing Editor, Elizabeth L. Hogan

Fifth printing May 1988

Contents

*Temptation at its best—a jar full of plump,
chewy Oatmeal Raisin Cookies (page 8).*

Special Features

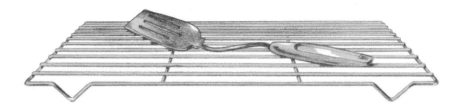

Cookie Craftsmanship

Trends in food come and go, but the popularity of cookies never wanes—easy to make, easy to eat, and appropriate for so many occasions, they're favorites with everyone.

The key to successful cookie baking is a thorough understanding of the ingredients, equipment, and techniques used in the process. The following tips will help you bake with confidence, turning out perfect cookies every time.

Ingredients

The ingredients used in cookie baking certainly aren't mysterious; butter, sugar, eggs, flour, leavenings, spices, and vanilla and other flavorings are familiar and widely available items. There are, however, a few things the baker should know when composing a shopping list.

For the shortening in most of our recipes, we call for butter *or* margarine. Butter gives cookies better flavor, but margarine may be substituted for dietary reasons. Some recipes—Spritz and Scottish Shortbread, for example—call for butter only; the flavor of butter is important in these cookies, and margarine should not be used.

When we call for brown sugar, we mean light (or "golden") brown sugar unless otherwise specified. If a recipe calls for honey, choose a mild-flavored variety such as clover or sage. Our recipes were tested using large eggs, and with real vanilla rather than imitation.

Many of our cookies call for peanut butter; you can use crunchy or creamy, unless the recipe indicates one style or the other. "Coconut" means packaged sweetened coconut; if unsweetened coconut is needed, the recipe specifically requests it. If you see "nuts" in an ingredient list, use almonds, walnuts, pecans, hazelnuts—whatever you have on hand or like best.

We use all-purpose flour in most of our cookies; either bleached or unbleached is fine. When rolled oats are called for, you can use either regular or quick-cooking unless the recipe indicates otherwise.

Techniques

In most of the recipes in this book, we use a standard technique for mixing cookie dough. You begin by beating butter and sugar until creamy, then beat in eggs, flavoring, and any liquid. Next, flour, leavening, salt, and any spices are stirred together and gradually beaten into the butter mixture. Nuts, chocolate chips, and other chunky ingredients are usually mixed in last of all, by hand.

Beating the butter and sugar until creamy is important for three reasons: to combine these ingredients thoroughly, to help the sugar start to dissolve, and to incorporate air into the dough for a light product. To achieve these goals, you must start with softened butter. Leave butter out of the refrigerator—or soften it in a microwave oven—until it reaches room temperature. (On the other hand, if the recipe calls for cutting the butter into dry ingredients, you'll need to use firm butter.)

Stir dry ingredients together in a bowl; it isn't necessary to sift them unless the recipe directs you to do so. It is important, however, to measure your dry ingredients carefully and accurately. Measure them in metal or plastic cups intended for dry ingredients, and use the cup that holds the exact amount called for in the recipe. Gently spoon the ingredient into the cup, piling it high and light; don't shake or pack it down. Then level off the top of the cup with a metal spatula or knife. Brown sugar is the exception to this rule; to measure it, pack it firmly into the cup with your fingers until it's even with the rim.

When you're ready to bake, always start out with cool baking sheets. If they're warm, the fat in the dough will begin to melt before the dough starts to bake, resulting in flat cookies. And don't grease sheets unless the recipe tells you to do so. Some cookies can't keep their "footing" on a greased sheet—they spread out and lose their shape as the grease melts.

Always preheat your oven before baking cookies. It's also a good idea to use an oven thermometer to make sure you're baking at the correct temperature. For best results, bake one sheet of cookies at a time, placing the baking sheet in the center of the oven and leaving at least an inch of space between the sides of the sheet and the oven wall.

After baking, transfer cookies to a rack to cool. Arrange them in a single layer, never stacked or overlapped; this lets air circulate around the hot cookies, allowing steam to evaporate and preventing cookies from becoming soggy. Let cookies cool completely before moving them.

Equipment

For mixing your cookie dough, an electric mixer is invaluable—though you can mix most doughs by hand, it takes much more time and effort. A mixer is a particularly worthwhile investment if you do a lot of baking; either a heavy-duty standing model or a small hand-held unit will give good service. You'll also want a rubber scraper and a sturdy wooden spoon to help in the mixing process. For grinding nuts, you'll need a blender or food processor.

To ensure accuracy, it's very important to have good measuring equipment. You'll need at least one set of measuring spoons, and separate measuring cups for liquid and dry ingredients.

For shaping the dough, have on hand a rolling pin, cookie cutters, and a sharp knife or pastry wheel. Some cookies require more specialized equipment, such as a cookie press, pastry bag, or cookie irons. For some recipes, you'll need wax paper, parchment paper, or plastic wrap.

Shiny, unrimmed baking sheets give the most evenly baked and browned cookies. Dark metal sheets retain heat, giving cookies dark (or even burned) bottoms; rimmed sheets make it harder for oven heat to reach cookies on all sides. You may also wish to try insulated baking sheets, made of two sheets of aluminum joined together with an air space in between. These do an especially good job of reducing the risk of burning.

A cooling rack (or racks) of wire or wood is a must for your finished cookies. Also have on hand a wide spatula for transferring cookies to the rack from baking sheets. Finally, you'll need utensils for decorating your cookies: a small spatula for spreading icing, a wire strainer or sifter for powdered sugar, a soft pastry brush for painting on melted chocolate and some glazes—and, occasionally, a pastry bag fitted with decorating tips.

Storage of Cookies

To preserve the freshly baked flavor and texture of your homemade cookies, store them airtight. This way, the moisture in the air won't soften crisp cookies, and soft cookies won't dry out. Unless otherwise specified in the recipe, cookies in this book will keep for about a week when stored airtight—depending, of course, on the climate and on what type of cookies they are.

What does airtight mean? Sealed plastic bags, tins, cookie jars with screw tops or gasket lids, rigid plastic storage containers, and sealed foil packets are all fine; separate layers with wax paper if the cookies are very moist or sticky. (If a recipe instructs you to store "covered" rather than "airtight," just cover cookies with plastic wrap or foil, making sure to secure the wrapping firmly around the edges of the plate or pan.)

Don't store cookies on loosely covered plates, in paper bags, or in boxes—these all allow air to circulate freely. And never store crisp cookies and soft cookies in the same container.

If you wish to keep your cookies for longer than a few days, consider freezing them. Cookies freeze beautifully, and will maintain oven-fresh quality for months if wrapped airtight first to prevent drying and freezer burn. If you freeze cookies that are frosted or glazed, be sure to thaw them unwrapped; otherwise, the icing may stick to the wrapping. (If possible, freeze the cookies unfrosted, then thaw and frost just before serving.) You can also freeze cookie dough, shaped or unshaped, for baking at a later time.

Heat-sealing offers a neat and attractive way of packaging cookies airtight; try it for large cookies that you want to give away as gifts or offer at a bake sale. To heat-seal, line a baking sheet with paper towels; put in a 325° oven. Wrap each cookie firmly in plastic wrap, taping at the back if necessary. Place cookies slightly apart on warm baking sheet without removing it from the oven; heat for about 2 minutes or until plastic shrinks tightly over cookies. Remove from oven and let cool.

Drop Cookies

So called because the dough is "dropped" by spoonfuls onto the baking sheets, drop cookies are generally simple, old-fashioned, and homey creations such as oatmeal raisin and chocolate chip. In fact, the very first cookie was a drop cookie—a small spoonful of cake batter, baked before the cake so that the cook could judge the oven temperature and the flavor and texture of the batter. The very word "cookie" comes from the Dutch *koekje,* meaning "little cake."

Today, drop cookies take a variety of forms. Though they're most often simple mounds studded with nuts or raisins or chocolate, they sometimes strike a more sophisticated pose—as in Chocolate-covered Almond Macaroons (page 15) and Florentines (page 16), for example.

Photo at left *presents a tempting collection of drop cookies. From top to bottom: Coconut-Macadamia Cookies (page 10); Blueberry Lemon Drops (page 13); Chocolate Cream Cushions (page 10); Mint Meringues (page 16); Brownie Date Drops (far left and far right; page 12); Coconut Macaroons (left and right center; page 15); Big Oatmeal Chocolate Chip Cookie (center; page 9); Mint Meringues, Chocolate Cream Cushions, Blueberry Lemon Drops, and Coconut-Macadamia Cookies.*

Oatmeal Raisin Cookies

(Pictured on page 3)

Oatmeal raisin drops are an ever-popular choice for lunchboxes, picnics, and after-school snacks. These are plump, chewy, and delightfully pebbled with oats, raisins, and nuts.

    1 **cup (½ lb.) butter or margarine, softened**
    2 **cups firmly packed brown sugar**
    2 **eggs**
    3 **tablespoons lemon juice**
    2 **cups all-purpose flour**
    1 **teaspoon** *each* **salt and baking soda**
    3 **cups quick-cooking rolled oats**
 1½ **cups raisins**
    1 **cup chopped walnuts**

In large bowl of an electric mixer, beat butter and sugar until creamy; then beat in eggs and lemon juice. In another bowl, stir together flour, salt, and baking soda; gradually add to butter mixture, blending thoroughly. Add oats, raisins, and walnuts and stir until well combined.

Drop dough by rounded tablespoonfuls onto ungreased baking sheets, spacing cookies about 2 inches apart. Bake in a 350° oven for 18 to 20 minutes or until edges are golden brown. Transfer to racks and let cool. Store airtight. Makes about 4 dozen.

Cream Cheese Gems

Creamy flavor and chewy texture distinguish these extravagantly rich little cookies.

 ½ **cup (¼ lb.) butter or margarine, softened**
  4 **ounces cream cheese, softened**
  1 **cup sugar**
 ½ **teaspoon** *each* **vanilla and grated lemon peel**
  1 **cup all-purpose flour**

In large bowl of an electric mixer, beat butter, cream cheese, and sugar until creamy; beat in vanilla and lemon peel. Gradually add flour, blending thoroughly.

Drop dough by rounded teaspoonfuls onto ungreased baking sheets, spacing cookies about 2 inches apart. Bake in a 350° oven for about 12 minutes or until edges are golden. Transfer to racks and let cool. Store airtight. Makes about 3½ dozen.

Addendum Cookies

Here's a drop cookie recipe with unlimited personality. After you make the basic dough, you stir in your choice of additions to decide the flavor and texture of the finished cookies. Since you divide the dough in half, you can make two distinctly different kinds of cookies from one batch.

    1 **cup (½ lb.) butter or margarine, softened**
    1 **cup** *each* **granulated sugar and firmly packed brown sugar**
    2 **eggs**
    2 **teaspoons vanilla**
 2½ **cups all-purpose flour**
    1 **teaspoon baking soda**
 ½ **teaspoon salt**
       Addenda (suggestions follow)

In large bowl of an electric mixer, beat butter, granulated sugar, and brown sugar until creamy; then beat in eggs and vanilla. In another bowl, stir together flour, baking soda, and salt; gradually add to butter mixture, blending thoroughly. Divide dough in half and mix one addendum into each portion; or double an addendum and mix it into the entire batch of dough.

Drop dough by rounded teaspoonfuls onto ungreased baking sheets, spacing cookies 2 inches apart. Bake in a 350° oven for 12 to 15 minutes or until just set in center when lightly touched. Transfer to racks and let cool. Store airtight. Makes 8 to 10 dozen.

Addenda. Stir one of the following into each half of the dough:

- 2 ounces **unsweetened chocolate,** melted and cooled, and ½ cup finely crushed **hard peppermint candy.**

- 2 ounces **unsweetened chocolate,** melted and cooled, 1½ teaspoons **rum flavoring,** and ½ cup crushed **peanut brittle** or chopped salted peanuts.

- ¼ cup **sour cream,** 1 teaspoon **ground nutmeg,** and ½ cup dry-roasted **sunflower seeds.**

- 1 cup **rolled oats,** 1 teaspoon grated **orange peel,** ¼ cup **orange juice,** and ½ cup **raisins** or snipped pitted dates.

- ½ cup **applesauce,** ½ cup **wheat germ** or crushed ready-to-eat cereal flakes, ½ cup chopped **nuts,** and 1 teaspoon **pumpkin pie spice** or ground cinnamon.

- 1 cup **granola-style cereal** (break up any large lumps before measuring), 1 cup snipped **pitted dates** or dried apricots, 1 teaspoon **ground cinnamon,** and ¼ cup **milk.**

Peanut Butter Platters

To give these giant peanut butter cookies the traditional crisscrossed tops of their smaller cousins, you can score them before baking with the tines of a fork or with a cake rack.

    1 **cup (½ lb.) butter or margarine, softened**
    1 **cup crunchy peanut butter**
    2 **cups firmly packed brown sugar**
    2 **eggs**
  2½ **cups all-purpose flour**
  1½ **teaspoons baking soda**
    1 **teaspoon baking powder**
    1 **cup chopped salted peanuts (optional)**
    Granulated sugar

In large bowl of an electric mixer, beat butter, peanut butter, and brown sugar until creamy; beat in eggs. In another bowl, stir together flour, baking soda, and baking powder; gradually add to butter mixture, blending thoroughly. Stir in peanuts, if desired.

To shape each cookie, spoon dough into a ½-cup measure, level off, and turn out onto a greased baking sheet. Space cookies at least 6 inches apart and 2½ inches from edge of baking sheet. Lightly grease the bottom of a pie pan, dip in granulated sugar, and use to flatten each cookie into a 5½-inch circle. If necessary, press cookies lightly with your fingers to give them an even thickness. If desired, make a crisscross pattern on top of cookies by lightly scoring with fork tines or pressing with a wire cake rack.

Bake in a 350° oven for about 14 minutes or until edges are lightly browned. Let cool on baking sheets for about 5 minutes; then transfer to racks and let cool completely. Store airtight. Makes 10 or 11.

Big Oatmeal Chocolate Chip Cookies

(Pictured on page 6)

Oversized cookies, often best-sellers at fund-raising events, are easy to make at home. Our Big Oatmeal Chocolate Chip Cookies, like our Peanut Butter Platters (preceding), reach a diameter of about 7 inches—enough cookie to last all day! For variety, you can use butterscotch-flavored chips instead of chocolate, or try the cinnamon-spiced raisin variation (see below).

    1 **cup (½ lb.) butter or margarine, softened**
  1½ **cups firmly packed brown sugar**
    2 **eggs**
    1 **teaspoon vanilla**
  1½ **cups all-purpose flour**
    2 **teaspoons baking soda**
    1 **teaspoon salt**
  2⅓ **cups rolled oats**
    1 **large package (12 oz.) semisweet chocolate or butterscotch-flavored chips**
  1½ **cups chopped nuts**
    Granulated sugar

In large bowl of an electric mixer, beat butter and brown sugar until creamy; then beat in eggs and vanilla. In another bowl, stir together flour, baking soda, and salt; gradually add to butter mixture, blending thoroughly. Add oats, chocolate chips, and nuts; stir until well combined.

To shape each cookie, spoon dough into a ½-cup measure, level off, and turn out onto a greased baking sheet. Space cookies at least 6 inches apart and 2½ inches from edge of baking sheet. Lightly grease the bottom of a pie pan, dip in granulated sugar, and use to flatten each cookie into a 5½-inch circle. If necessary, press cookies lightly with your fingers to give them an even thickness.

Bake in a 350° oven for about 15 minutes or until edges are lightly browned. Let cool on baking sheets for about 5 minutes; then transfer to racks and let cool completely. Store airtight. Makes about 1 dozen.

Big Oatmeal Raisin Cookies

Follow directions for **Big Oatmeal Chocolate Chip Cookies,** but add 1 teaspoon **ground cinnamon** and ½ teaspoon **ground nutmeg** with flour. Omit chocolate chips and add 1½ cups **raisins.**

Chocolate Chip Cookies at Their Best

(Pictured on facing page and on front cover)

The cook who invented these special cookies was obviously following William Blake's dictum, "the road to excess leads to the palace of wisdom"— they're large and chock-full of chocolate and nuts. Bake them one way if you like your cookies soft and chewy, another way if you prefer them crisp.

- 1 cup (½ lb.) butter or margarine, softened
- ½ cup solid vegetable shortening
- 1⅓ cups granulated sugar
- 1 cup firmly packed brown sugar
- 4 eggs
- 1 tablespoon vanilla
- 1 teaspoon lemon juice
- 3 cups all-purpose flour
- 2 teaspoons baking soda
- 1½ teaspoons salt
- 1 teaspoon ground cinnamon (optional)
- ½ cup rolled oats
- 2 large packages (12 oz. *each*) semisweet chocolate chips
- 2 cups chopped walnuts

In large bowl of an electric mixer, beat butter, shortening, granulated sugar, and brown sugar on high speed until very light and fluffy (about 5 minutes). Add eggs, one at a time, beating well after each addition. Beat in vanilla and lemon juice. In another bowl, stir together flour, baking soda, salt, cinnamon (if used), and oats. Gradually add to butter mixture, blending thoroughly. Stir in chocolate chips and walnuts.

Use a scant ¼ cup of dough for each cookie. Drop dough onto lightly greased baking sheets, spacing cookies about 3 inches apart. For soft cookies, bake in a 325° oven for 17 to 19 minutes or until light golden brown; for crisp cookies, bake in a 350° oven for 16 to 18 minutes or until golden brown. Transfer to racks and let cool. Store airtight. Makes about 3 dozen.

Coconut-Macadamia Cookies

(Pictured on page 6)

Follow directions for **Chocolate Chip Cookies at Their Best,** but use ⅔ cup granulated sugar and 1⅔ cups firmly packed brown sugar; increase flour to 3½ cups and omit cinnamon and oats. Omit chocolate chips and walnuts; instead, stir in 2½ cups **shredded coconut** and 1½ cups very coarsely chopped **macadamia nuts.** Bake in a 325° oven for 22 to 25 minutes or until golden brown.

Chocolate Cream Cushions

(Pictured on page 6)

Depending on what flavor you fancy, you can fill these soft chocolate sandwich cookies with vanilla, peppermint, or peanut buttercream.

- 6 tablespoons butter or margarine, softened
- 1 cup sugar
- 1 egg
- 1 teaspoon vanilla
- 2 cups all-purpose flour
- 1¼ teaspoons baking soda
- ¼ teaspoon salt
- 5 tablespoons unsweetened cocoa
- 1 cup milk
- Buttercream (recipes follow)

In large bowl of an electric mixer, beat butter and sugar until creamy; beat in egg and vanilla. In another bowl, stir together flour, baking soda, salt, and cocoa; add to butter mixture alternately with milk, beating just until smooth.

Drop dough by rounded teaspoonfuls onto greased baking sheets, spacing cookies about 2 inches apart. Bake in a 400° oven for 10 minutes or until firm when lightly touched. Transfer to racks and let cool completely. Meanwhile, prepare your choice of buttercream.

Spread bottoms of half the cooled cookies with buttercream; top with remaining cookies, top side up. Store airtight. Makes about 2½ dozen.

Vanilla buttercream. In small bowl of an electric mixer, beat until smooth: ¾ cup (¼ lb. plus 4 tablespoons) **butter** or margarine (softened), ¾ cup **powdered sugar,** 6 tablespoons **marshmallow creme,** and 1 teaspoon **vanilla.**

Peppermint buttercream. Follow directions for **Vanilla buttercream,** but use 1 teaspoon **peppermint extract** in place of vanilla.

Peanut buttercream. Follow directions for **Vanilla buttercream,** but substitute ½ cup **peanut butter** for ½ cup of the butter. Omit vanilla.

Chocolate Chip Cookies at Their Best *(Recipe on facing page)*

1 Beat sugar mixture until very light and fluffy to combine thoroughly, and to incorporate air.

2 Chop nuts with a large knife, lifting heel of knife in up-and-down movements and steadying tip of blade with other hand.

3 Chopped nuts and chocolate chips are stirred in by hand after other ingredients are well combined.

4 For each cookie, drop a scant ¼ cup dough onto lightly greased baking sheet.

Brownie Date Drops

(Pictured on page 6)

Chewy and chocolaty as a brownie, these soft drops are studded with dates and walnuts for extra-special flavor and texture.

½ cup (¼ lb.) **butter or margarine, softened**
1 **cup sugar**
2 **eggs**
1 **teaspoon vanilla**
2 **ounces unsweetened chocolate, melted and cooled**
1 **cup all-purpose flour**
1 **teaspoon baking powder**
½ **teaspoon salt**
1 **cup** *each* **snipped pitted dates and chopped walnuts**

In large bowl of an electric mixer, beat butter and sugar until creamy; beat in eggs and vanilla, then chocolate. In another bowl, stir together flour, baking powder, and salt; gradually add to butter mixture, blending thoroughly. Stir in dates and walnuts.

Drop dough by level tablespoonfuls onto greased baking sheets, spacing cookies about 1 inch apart. Bake in a 350° oven for 13 minutes or until tops are dry and just set when lightly touched (cookies will be soft; do not overbake). Transfer to racks and let cool. Store airtight. Makes about 3 dozen.

Clove Cookies

One doesn't often find drop cookies of the crisp, buttery variety, but these clove-spiced morsels are just that. Serve them with hot tea on a winter's afternoon—or with lemonade in summer.

½ cup (¼ lb.) **butter**
1 **cup sugar**
1 **teaspoon vanilla**
1 **egg**
1 **cup all-purpose flour**
1 **teaspoon ground cloves**

Melt butter in a small pan over medium heat. Remove from heat and stir in sugar until well combined; then stir in vanilla. Add egg and beat until mixture is smooth. In a small bowl, stir together flour and cloves; gradually add to butter mixture, blending thoroughly.

Drop dough by level teaspoonfuls onto well-greased baking sheets, spacing cookies 2½ to 3 inches apart. Bake in a 350° oven for 12 to 14 minutes or until edges are golden brown and puffy tops start to crinkle and collapse. Immediately transfer cookies to racks and let cool. Store airtight. Makes about 4 dozen.

Frosted Apple Drops

A plateful of these soft, frosted apple cookies is sure to please on an autumn afternoon—or any other time. The spicy cookies are studded with raisins and chunks of apple.

½ cup (¼ lb.) **butter or margarine, softened**
1⅓ **cups firmly packed brown sugar**
1 **egg**
2 **cups all-purpose flour**
1 **teaspoon** *each* **baking soda and ground cinnamon**
½ **teaspoon** *each* **salt, ground cloves, and ground nutmeg**
¼ **cup apple juice or milk**
1 **cup** *each* **raisins and peeled, finely chopped apples**
Apple frosting (recipe follows)

In large bowl of an electric mixer, beat butter and sugar until creamy; beat in egg. In another bowl, stir together flour, baking soda, cinnamon, salt, cloves, and nutmeg. Add flour mixture to butter mixture alternately with apple juice, mixing well after each addition; stir in raisins and apples.

Drop dough by level tablespoonfuls onto well-greased baking sheets, spacing cookies about 2 inches apart. Bake in a 400° oven for about 10 minutes or until golden brown. Transfer to racks. Prepare apple frosting and spread over cookies while they're still slightly warm. Let cool completely. Store airtight. Makes about 4½ dozen.

Apple frosting. In a bowl, beat 2 tablespoons **butter** or margarine (softened) and 1½ cups sifted **powdered sugar** until creamy. Beat in ¼ teaspoon **vanilla,** a dash of **salt,** and enough **apple juice** or milk (about 2 tablespoons) to obtain a good spreading consistency.

Maple Graham Crisps

Graham cracker crumbs and maple flavoring give these golden cookies their warm, sweet flavor. They're rich and buttery, with an appealingly crisp texture—good cookies to serve with a glass of cold milk. Use purchased cracker crumbs or whirl your own in a food processor or blender.

> 1 cup (½ lb.) butter or margarine, softened
> 1 cup sugar
> 1 egg
> 1 teaspoon maple flavoring
> 1¼ cups fine graham cracker crumbs (about 20 squares)
> 1 cup all-purpose flour

In large bowl of an electric mixer, beat butter and sugar until creamy; then beat in egg and maple flavoring. Gradually add graham cracker crumbs and flour, blending thoroughly. Cover tightly with plastic wrap and refrigerate until firm (at least 1 hour).

Drop dough by rounded teaspoonfuls onto ungreased baking sheets, spacing cookies about 2 inches apart. (Keep any remaining dough refrigerated until you're ready to use it.) Bake in a 325° oven for 16 to 18 minutes or until firm when lightly touched. Let cool on baking sheets for 1 to 2 minutes, then transfer to racks and let cool completely. Store airtight. Makes about 4 dozen.

Bourbon Chews

These cookies are spirited in more ways than one. Molasses and ginger provide part of their spicy character; bourbon whiskey does the rest.

> 1 cup all-purpose flour
> ½ cup sugar
> 1 teaspoon ground ginger
> ¼ teaspoon salt
> ⅓ cup light molasses
> ½ cup (¼ lb.) butter or margarine
> 3 tablespoons bourbon whiskey
> ¼ cup chopped almonds or walnuts

In a small bowl, stir together flour, sugar, ginger, and salt; set aside. In a 1-quart pan, bring molasses to a boil over high heat; add butter and stir until melted. Remove from heat and stir in flour mixture, bourbon, and almonds until batter is smooth and well combined.

Drop batter by level tablespoonfuls onto greased baking sheets, spacing cookies about 3 inches apart; then spread each into a 2-inch circle with the back of a spoon. Bake in a 300° oven for 8 to 10 minutes or until cookies look dry and are no longer sticky to the touch. Let cool on baking sheets for about 3 minutes, then transfer to racks and let cool completely. Store airtight. Makes about 2 dozen.

Blueberry Lemon Drops

(Pictured on page 6)

Here's a summertime treat made with fresh blueberries—a sugar-dusted drop cookie that resembles a blueberry muffin in its soft, cakelike appeal. The cookies are at their prime of fragrance and juiciness while still warm, so plan to eat them soon after baking. If you like, you can prepare the dough in advance and refrigerate it, then bake the cookies at the last minute.

> ½ cup (¼ lb.) butter or margarine, softened
> 1 cup granulated sugar
> 1½ teaspoons grated lemon peel
> 1 egg
> 2 cups all-purpose flour
> 2 teaspoons baking powder
> ½ teaspoon salt
> ¼ cup milk
> 1 cup fresh blueberries
> Powdered sugar

In large bowl of an electric mixer, beat butter until creamy; gradually add granulated sugar, beating until smoothly blended. Beat in lemon peel and egg. In another bowl, stir together flour, baking powder, and salt; add to butter mixture alternately with milk, blending thoroughly. Gently stir in blueberries.

Drop dough by rounded tablespoonfuls onto greased baking sheets, spacing cookies about 2 inches apart. Bake in a 375° oven for about 15 minutes or until golden brown. Transfer to racks and let cool for 5 minutes; then sift powdered sugar lightly over tops. Serve warm, or let cool completely and store airtight for up to 3 days. Makes about 3 dozen.

Chocolate-covered Almond Macaroons *(Recipe on facing page)*

1 Fold ground almond mixture, a third at a time, into beaten egg whites.

2 Use a spoon, a small rubber scraper, or a finger to nudge batter onto parchment-lined baking sheets.

3 Spread chocolate buttercream over flat bottom of each macaroon; then refrigerate until buttercream is firm.

4 Dip buttercream side of each cookie into chocolate. Refrigerate until coating is set.

14 Drop Cookies

Chocolate-covered Almond Macaroons

(Pictured on facing page)

In Swedish *konditorier* (pastry shops), you'll find a rich and irresistible confection: almond macaroons topped with chocolate buttercream and dipped in semisweet chocolate. Though they take a little more time to make than the average cookie, these elegant morsels are well worth the trouble when the occasion calls for something special—and you can make them well in advance, then refrigerate or freeze them.

> **Almond macaroons (recipe follows)**
> **Chocolate buttercream (recipe follows)**
> 5 ounces semisweet chocolate
> 1 tablespoon plus 2 teaspoons solid vegetable shortening

Prepare macaroons and let cool completely. Prepare buttercream and spread one tablespoonful over bottom of each cooled cookie. Then place cookies, buttercream side up, in a single layer on a pan or plate and refrigerate until buttercream is firm (at least 15 minutes).

Meanwhile, place chocolate and shortening in the top of a double boiler over simmering water; stir just until melted. Transfer chocolate mixture to a small, shallow bowl for easier handling and let cool, stirring occasionally, until lukewarm (80° to 85° F).

Hold each cookie buttercream side down and dip in chocolate to coat buttercream. Then place cookies on a pan or plate, chocolate side up, and refrigerate until chocolate coating is set (at least 10 minutes). When chocolate is firm, cover cookies lightly and store in the refrigerator for up to 3 days. (Freeze for longer storage; let thaw in refrigerator for at least 3 hours before serving.) Makes about 1½ dozen.

Almond macaroons. In a blender or food processor, whirl 1½ cups **whole blanched almonds** until finely ground. Place in a bowl and add 1½ cups sifted **powdered sugar**; stir until mixture is free from lumps.

Separate 3 eggs. Reserve yolks for buttercream; place **egg whites** in a bowl and beat just until moist, stiff peaks form. Then sprinkle almond mixture over egg whites, a third at a time, folding in each addition until blended.

Drop mixture by rounded tablespoonfuls onto baking sheets lined with parchment paper, spacing cookies about 1 inch apart. Bake in a 350° oven for 15 to 18 minutes or until lightly browned. Let cool on baking sheets for about 5 minutes, then transfer to racks with a wide spatula. Let cool.

Chocolate buttercream. In a small pan, stir together 7 tablespoons *each* **sugar** and **water**. Bring to a boil over high heat; continue to boil until syrup reaches 230° to 234° F on a candy thermometer (or until syrup spins a 2-inch thread when dropped from a fork or spoon).

In small bowl of an electric mixer, beat **4 egg yolks** until blended. Beating constantly, slowly add hot syrup in a thin, steady stream; beat until mixture is thick and lemon-colored and has cooled to room temperature. Then beat in ⅔ cup **butter** (softened), a tablespoon at a time, just until blended. Stir in 4 teaspoons **unsweetened cocoa.** (If mixture gets dark and runny from overbeating, refrigerate it, then beat again.)

Coconut Macaroons

(Pictured on page 6)

Traditionally, macaroons are made from egg whites, sugar, and ground almonds (see preceding recipe) or almond paste (see Swiss Almond Macaroons, page 55). Sometimes, however, coconut makes an appearance to provide a rich and chewy variation. If you'd like to enjoy the flavor of both almond and coconut in the same macaroon, try substituting almond extract for the vanilla in this recipe; that way, you can enjoy the best of both worlds.

> 4 egg whites
> ¼ teaspoon salt
> ⅔ cup sugar
> 1 teaspoon vanilla
> ¼ cup all-purpose flour
> 3 cups lightly packed flaked coconut

In large bowl of an electric mixer, beat egg whites until foamy; beat in salt, sugar, vanilla, and flour. Add coconut and stir until well combined.

Drop batter by rounded teaspoonfuls onto well-greased baking sheets, spacing cookies about 1 inch apart. Bake in a 325° oven for 20 to 25 minutes or until lightly browned. Let cool briefly on baking sheets, then transfer to racks and let cool completely. Store airtight. Makes about 3 dozen.

Mint Meringues

(Pictured on page 6)

These light, dainty cookies are flavored with mint and studded with chocolate chips. If you like, you can give them a festive holiday look by tinting them with green or red food color.

      2 **egg whites**
    ½ **cup sugar**
    ½ **teaspoon peppermint or spearmint extract**
      6 **to 8 drops green or red food color (optional)**
      1 **package (6 oz.) semisweet chocolate chips**

In large bowl of an electric mixer, beat egg whites until foamy. With mixer on high speed, gradually add sugar, about a tablespoon at a time, beating well after each addition, until whites hold stiff, glossy peaks. Add peppermint extract and food color (if used); beat for 1 more minute. Fold in chocolate chips.

Drop meringue mixture by rounded teaspoonfuls onto well-greased baking sheets, spacing cookies about 1 inch apart. Bake in a 200° oven for 1 hour or until outside is dry and set; cookies should not turn brown. Let cool on baking sheets for about 5 minutes, then transfer to racks and let cool completely. Store airtight. Makes about 3½ dozen.

Date-nut Meringues

If you've got a couple of extra egg whites, put them to delicious use in these chewy little datenut nuggets.

      2 **egg whites**
         Dash of salt
    ½ **cup sugar**
      1 **teaspoon vanilla**
      1 **cup *each* snipped pitted dates and finely chopped walnuts**

In large bowl of an electric mixer, beat egg whites until foamy. With mixer on high speed, beat in salt; then gradually add sugar, about a tablespoon at a time, beating well after each addition, until whites hold stiff, glossy peaks. Add vanilla and beat for 1 more minute. Fold in dates and walnuts.

Drop meringue mixture by rounded teaspoonfuls onto well-greased baking sheets, spacing cookies about 1 inch apart. Bake in a 200° oven for 1 hour or until outside is dry and set; cookies should not turn brown. Let cool on baking sheets for about 5 minutes, then transfer to racks and let cool completely. Store airtight. Makes about 3½ dozen.

Florentines

Rich and chewy Florentines are truly a dessert cookie, best served in the evening with coffee or tea. They're flavored with almonds and candied orange peel, and painted on one side with semisweet chocolate.

      1 **cup sliced almonds**
    ¼ **cup whipping cream**
    ⅓ **cup sugar**
      4 **tablespoons butter or margarine**
    ½ **cup candied orange peel, finely chopped**
      2 **tablespoons all-purpose flour**
      4 **ounces semisweet chocolate**
      4 **teaspoons solid vegetable shortening**

In a blender or food processor, whirl ½ cup of the almonds until finely ground. Set aside.

Combine cream, sugar, and butter in a medium-size pan and cook over low heat, stirring occasionally, until butter is melted. Increase heat to medium-high and bring mixture to a boil; then remove from heat and stir in ground almonds, remaining ½ cup sliced almonds, orange peel, and flour. Batter will be very thin.

Drop batter by level tablespoonfuls onto lightly greased and flour-dusted baking sheets, spacing cookies 3 inches apart; then spread each into a 2-inch circle with the back of a spoon. Bake in a 350° oven for 10 to 12 minutes or until edges are lightly browned (centers will still be bubbling). Let cool on baking sheets for 1 to 2 minutes, then carefully transfer to racks with a wide spatula and let cool completely.

Turn cooled cookies upside down on a piece of wax paper. Place chocolate and shortening in top of a double boiler over simmering water; stir until melted. With a soft pastry brush, paint a thin layer of chocolate over bottom of each cookie. Refrigerate until chocolate has hardened; then cover lightly and store in the refrigerator for up to 3 days. Makes about 15.

Packing & Sending Cookies

Sending homemade cookies to friends and loved ones in faraway places is a sure way of showing your affection, no matter what the occasion. Birthdays, holidays, and college exam weeks are perhaps the most popular times for sending cookie gifts, but why wait for a special event? Cookies are a welcome sight any time.

Which Cookies to Send

Make sure you select cookies that are good travelers. They must be sturdy enough to make the journey, and must keep well enough to stay fresh until they arrive at their destination. Don't choose anything fragile (Krumkake, for example), or it may be crushed in transit. Also avoid sticky cookies or those with moist icings or frostings. Crisp cookies are fine if they're not too delicate or crumbly, but the most reliable travelers are firm but not brittle cookies.

The cookies listed below are especially good candidates for mailing.

Wrapping, Packing & Mailing

Cookies can be wrapped for travel in several ways. You can wrap them in foil—either individually, in pairs (flat sides together), or in small stacks. Or layer the cookies in containers, such as pretty tins, rigid plastic containers, or attractively wrapped foil loaf or pie pans. Separate layers with wax paper, and pack the cookies securely so they won't jostle about and damage each other in transit. If the container you've chosen isn't airtight, seal it in a plastic bag.

However you wrap your cookies, be sure to pack soft and crisp ones separately to preserve their textures.

To pack the cookies for mailing, you'll need a stout box lined with foil or wax paper, and plenty of filler for insulation. For filler, use tightly crumpled newspaper or other paper (colored tissue paper gives a festive appearance) or styrofoam packing material. Pad the bottom of the box with several inches of filler; then start adding cookies, making sure to insulate well with filler between packages and around the sides of the box. Add several inches of filler on top of the cookies before closing the box.

The post office requires that all packages be sealed securely with reinforced packing tape; don't use masking tape or transparent tape or tie your package with string. Send the package first-class so that your cookies will arrive promptly.

Bar Cookies

Sometimes chewy, sometimes cakey, and sometimes crisp and crunchy, bar cookies are always popular— and because they're quick to prepare, they're often favorites with the cook, too. The key to their speedy preparation is the fact that they're spread in a pan and baked all at once, rather than being individually shaped. This also makes them good candidates for taking to picnics and parties—you can wrap and carry them easily, right in their baking pans.

The recipes in this chapter run the gamut from classics like Fudge Brownies (page 21) to more unusual creations such as Bee Sting Bars (page 24) and Cheesecake Squares (page 29). For best results, always use the pan size specified in the recipe: we most often call for 8 or 9-inch square, 9 by 13-inch, or 10 by 15-inch. After baking, the cookies may be cut into squares, rectangles, or triangles—or, in some cases, just broken into irregular chunks.

Photo at right displays a mosaic of delectable bar cookies. Separating the sections: Dream Bars (page 29). Others, clockwise from upper right: Fudge Brownies (page 21), Buttery Lemon Bars (page 20), Banana Squares (page 20), Chocolate Oatmeal Peanut Bars (page 21), and Bee Sting Bars (page 24).

Banana Squares

(Pictured on page 19)

Paired with cold milk, these banana-flavored treats are the perfect thing to satisfy after-school appetites. Each square is studded with butterscotch chips (or raisins, if you prefer).

    6 tablespoons butter or margarine, softened
    1 cup firmly packed brown sugar
    1 egg
    ½ teaspoon vanilla
    1 large banana, mashed
    1¾ cups all-purpose flour
    1½ teaspoons baking powder
    ½ teaspoon salt
    ½ cup chopped walnuts
    1 package (6 oz.) butterscotch-flavored chips
       or 1 cup raisins

In large bowl of an electric mixer, beat butter and sugar until creamy; beat in egg, vanilla, and banana. In another bowl, stir together flour, baking powder, and salt; gradually add to butter mixture, blending thoroughly. Stir in walnuts and butterscotch chips.

Spread batter evenly in a greased 9-inch square baking pan. Bake in a 350° oven for 35 to 40 minutes or until golden brown. Let cool in pan on a rack, then cut into 2¼-inch squares. Store airtight. Makes 16.

Buttery Lemon Bars

(Pictured on page 19)

These luscious bars will remind you of lemon meringue pie—minus the meringue topping, and with a cookie crust instead of pie pastry.

    1 cup (½ lb.) butter or margarine, softened
    ½ cup powdered sugar
    2⅓ cups all-purpose flour
    4 eggs
    2 cups granulated sugar
    1 teaspoon grated lemon peel
    6 tablespoons lemon juice
    1 teaspoon baking powder
       Powdered sugar

In large bowl of an electric mixer, beat butter and the ½ cup powdered sugar until creamy; beat in 2 cups of the flour, blending thoroughly. Spread mixture evenly over bottom of a well-greased 9 by 13-inch baking pan. Bake in a 350° oven for 20 minutes.

Meanwhile, in small bowl of mixer, beat eggs until light. Gradually add granulated sugar, beating until mixture is thick and lemon-colored. Add lemon peel, lemon juice, remaining ⅓ cup flour, and baking powder; beat until smooth and well combined.

Pour lemon mixture over baked crust and return to oven; bake for 15 to 20 minutes or until topping is pale golden. Place on a rack to cool; while still warm, sift powdered sugar lightly over top. To serve, cut into bars about 2¼ by 2½ inches. Store airtight. Makes about 20.

Lemon-Coconut Dessert Bars

A buttery coconut crumb crust conceals the piquant lemon filling of these rich bars. They belong to a versatile group of desserts somewhere between cookies and cake—you can cut them into cookie-size pieces to eat out of hand, or serve larger portions on small plates, to eat with forks.

    2 cups all-purpose flour
    1 cup sugar
    1 teaspoon *each* baking powder and grated
       lemon peel
    9 tablespoons (¼ lb. plus 1 tablespoon) firm
       butter or margarine, cut into pieces
    1 cup flaked coconut
    2 egg yolks
       Lemon filling (recipe follows)

In a large mixing bowl, stir together flour, sugar, baking powder, and lemon peel. Add butter and rub in with your fingers until mixture resembles cornmeal. Add coconut and egg yolks and blend thoroughly.

Spoon a little more than half the coconut mixture into a lightly greased 9-inch square baking pan. Press gently and evenly over bottom of pan. Bake in a 350° oven for 15 minutes. Meanwhile, prepare lemon filling.

Remove pan from oven; pour lemon filling over crust and spread to edges of pan. Sprinkle remaining coconut mixture evenly over top; spread with a fork to level, then pat down gently. Return to oven and bake for 20 to 25 minutes or until lightly browned. Let cool completely in pan on a rack; then cut into bars about 1¾ by 3 inches. Store, covered, for up to 4 days. Makes about 15.

Lemon filling. In a small pan, stir together ½ cup **sugar** and 2½ tablespoons **cornstarch.** Gradually stir in 1 cup **water.** Bring to a full boil over medium-high heat, stirring; cook, stirring constantly, for 1 minute (mixture will be very thick). Remove from heat; add 2 tablespoons **butter** or margarine, ⅓ cup **lemon juice,** and 1½ teaspoons grated **lemon peel.** Stir until butter is melted.

Chocolate Oatmeal Peanut Bars

(Pictured on page 19)

Chocolate and peanuts are a tempting combination, especially in these chewy, candylike bar cookies. They feature a creamy topping of chocolate and peanut butter over an oatmeal crust; a sprinkling of chopped peanuts makes a decorative crowning touch.

>   ⅔ cup butter or margarine, softened
>   ½ cup firmly packed brown sugar
>   ½ cup light corn syrup
>   2 teaspoons vanilla
>   4 cups quick-cooking rolled oats
>   1 package (6 oz.) semisweet chocolate chips
>   ⅔ cup creamy peanut butter
>   ⅓ cup chopped dry-roasted peanuts

In large bowl of an electric mixer, beat butter and sugar until creamy; stir in corn syrup, vanilla, and oats, blending thoroughly. Pat dough evenly over bottom of a greased 9 by 13-inch baking pan. Bake in a 350° oven for about 20 minutes or until golden around edges; let cool in pan on a rack, then cover and refrigerate until cold.

   Meanwhile, place chocolate chips and peanut butter in a 1½ to 2-quart pan. Stir over very low heat until melted and smooth. Spread mixture evenly over baked crust; sprinkle with peanuts. Refrigerate until topping firms slightly (about 15 minutes); then cut into bars about 1 by 2 inches. Store, covered, in refrigerator. Makes about 4½ dozen.

Fudge Brownies

(Pictured on page 19)

Brownies are always winners, and this fudgy version will keep you coming back for more.

>   ½ cup (¼ lb.) butter or margarine
>   4 ounces unsweetened chocolate
>   2 cups sugar
>   1½ teaspoons vanilla
>   4 eggs
>   1 cup all-purpose flour
>   ½ to 1 cup coarsely chopped walnuts

In a 2 to 3-quart pan, melt butter and chocolate over medium-low heat, stirring until well blended. Remove from heat and stir in sugar and vanilla. Add eggs, one at a time, beating well after each addition. Stir in flour; then mix in walnuts.

   Spread batter evenly in a greased 9-inch square baking pan. Bake in a 325° oven for about 35 minutes or until brownie feels dry on top. Let cool in pan on a rack, then cut into 2¼-inch squares. Store airtight. Makes 16.

Butterscotch Brownies

Sometimes called "blondies," these chewy squares are made with butter and brown sugar for a rich flavor and a handsome golden hue.

>   4 tablespoons butter or margarine
>   1 cup firmly packed brown sugar
>   1 egg
>   1 teaspoon vanilla
>   1 cup all-purpose flour
>   1 teaspoon baking powder
>   ½ teaspoon salt
>   ¼ cup chopped walnuts or pecans

Melt butter in a medium-size pan over medium heat. Remove from heat and stir in sugar; add egg and vanilla and beat until well combined. Stir in flour, baking powder, salt and walnuts.

   Spread batter evenly in a greased 8-inch square baking pan; bake in a 375° oven for 20 to 25 minutes or until golden brown. Let cool in pan on a rack, then cut into 2-inch squares. Store airtight. Makes 16.

Triple-layered Brownie Squares *(Recipe on facing page)*

1 In the top of a double boiler over simmering water, melt chocolate and butter.

2 Turn brownie batter into a lightly greased 9-inch square baking pan. Spread out in an even layer.

3 Spread vanilla frosting evenly over baked and cooled brownie to make second layer.

4 Drizzle chocolate glaze over frosting and tilt pan so chocolate covers surface evenly.

Triple-layered Brownie Squares

(Pictured on facing page)

Gilding the lily may not be good taste in art, but for a brownie the standards are different. Dieters beware: here you bake a thin, nut-laden brownie, spread a vanilla frosting over it, and then top it all with a dark chocolate icing. For variety, you may also want to try our mint variation (below).

    2 ounces unsweetened chocolate
    ¾ cup (¼ lb. plus 4 tablespoons) butter
        or margarine
    1 egg
    ½ cup granulated sugar
    ¼ cup all-purpose flour
    1 cup chopped almonds or pecans
    2 cups powdered sugar
    ½ teaspoon vanilla
    2 to 3 tablespoons whipping cream

For the first layer, place 1 ounce of the chocolate and 4 tablespoons of the butter in the top of a double boiler over simmering water (or in a small pan over lowest possible heat). Stir until melted.

In a small mixing bowl, beat egg and granulated sugar, then gradually beat in chocolate mixture. Stir in flour and almonds. Spread batter evenly in a lightly greased 9-inch square baking pan; bake in a 350° oven for 20 to 25 minutes or until brownie feels dry on top. Let cool completely in pan on a rack.

For the second layer, place 4 tablespoons of the butter, powdered sugar, and vanilla in small bowl of an electric mixer. Beat together; then beat in enough cream to make frosting spreadable. Spread evenly over cooled brownie.

For the third layer, combine remaining 1 ounce chocolate and remaining 4 tablespoons butter in the top of a double boiler over simmering water (or in a small pan over lowest possible heat). Stir until melted. Drizzle over frosting layer; tilt pan so chocolate covers surface evenly. Refrigerate until chocolate is hardened (about 15 minutes). Cut into 2¼-inch squares. Store, covered, in refrigerator. Makes 16.

Mint-layered Brownie Squares

Follow directions for **Triple-layered Brownie Squares,** but add 1 teaspoon **peppermint extract** to frosting (second layer).

Applesauce-Raisin Brownies

(Pictured on front cover)

Not all brownies are dark and chocolaty, as this recipe proves. It produces old-fashioned "brownies" that are much like spice cake—light-textured, dotted with raisins and nuts, and flavored with cinnamon and nutmeg. Applesauce makes them moist; an orange butter frosting lends a special, fancy touch.

If you have a citrus zester, you can use it to make fine strands of orange peel for decorating the brownies.

    6 tablespoons butter or margarine
    1¼ cups firmly packed brown sugar
    ½ cup applesauce
    1 egg
    1 teaspoon vanilla
    1¼ cups all-purpose flour
    1 teaspoon baking powder
    ½ teaspoon *each* salt and ground cinnamon
    ¼ teaspoon *each* baking soda and ground
        nutmeg
    ½ cup *each* raisins and chopped nuts
        Orange frosting (optional; recipe follows)
        Orange zest (optional)

Melt butter in a small pan over medium-low heat. Remove from heat and stir in sugar; then stir in applesauce, egg, and vanilla. In a bowl, stir together flour, baking powder, salt, cinnamon, baking soda, and nutmeg; add applesauce mixture and blend thoroughly. Add raisins and nuts; stir until well combined.

Spread batter evenly in a greased 9 by 13-inch baking pan. Bake in a 350° oven for 25 minutes or until a pick inserted in center comes out clean. Let cool completely in pan on a rack. If desired, prepare orange frosting and spread over cooled brownie; then garnish with orange zest. Cut into bars (about 1½ by 3 inches) or squares (about 2¼ by 2¼ inches). Store covered. Makes about 2 dozen.

Orange frosting. In small bowl of an electric mixer, beat together until smooth: 1¾ cups **powdered sugar;** 2½ tablespoons **butter** or margarine, softened; 2 tablespoons **milk;** and ½ teaspoon **vanilla.** Beat in ½ teaspoon grated **orange peel.** If necessary, beat in a few more drops milk to make a good spreading consistency.

English Toffee Squares

When you need a dessert for a large gathering, you'll appreciate this recipe. With little effort, you can produce six dozen delicious and easily portable toffee-flavored bar cookies.

> 1 cup (½ lb.) butter or margarine, softened
> 1 cup sugar
> 1 egg
> 2 cups all-purpose flour
> 1 teaspoon ground cinnamon
> 1 cup chopped pecans or walnuts

In large bowl of an electric mixer, beat butter and sugar until creamy. Separate egg. Beat yolk into butter mixture; cover and reserve white.

In another bowl, stir together flour and cinnamon; add to butter mixture, using your hands if necessary to blend thoroughly.

With your hands, spread dough evenly over bottom of a greased 10 by 15-inch rimmed baking pan. Beat egg white lightly, then brush over dough to cover evenly. Sprinkle pecans over top; press in lightly.

Bake in a 275° oven for 1 hour or until firm when lightly touched. While still hot, cut into 1½-inch squares. Let cool in pan on a rack. Store airtight. Makes about 6 dozen.

Bee Sting Bars

(Pictured on page 19)

These fancifully named honey-almond bars come from Germany, where they're known as *Bienenstich*.

> 1 cup (½ lb.) firm butter or margarine
> ¾ cup sugar
> 2 tablespoons *each* honey and milk
> 1 cup chopped or slivered almonds
> 1 teaspoon almond extract
> 1¾ cups all-purpose flour
> 2 teaspoons baking powder
> ¼ teaspoon salt
> 1 egg

In a small pan, combine ½ cup of the butter, ¼ cup of the sugar, honey, milk, almonds, and almond

extract. Bring to a rolling boil over medium-high heat, stirring; set aside.

In a mixing bowl, stir together flour, remaining ½ cup sugar, baking powder, and salt. Cut remaining ½ cup butter into pieces and, with a pastry blender or 2 knives, cut into flour mixture until mixture is very crumbly and no large particles remain. Add egg and mix with a fork until dough holds together.

Press dough evenly over bottom of an ungreased 10 by 15-inch rimmed baking pan. Pour almond mixture over dough, spreading evenly. Bake in a 350° oven for 20 to 25 minutes or until topping is deep golden. Let cool in pan on a rack. Cut into 2-inch squares; for smaller cookies, cut each square diagonally into 2 triangles. Store airtight. Makes about 3 dozen squares or about 6 dozen triangles.

Italian Crumb Cookie

A specialty of Veneto, Italy, this giant break-apart cookie starts as a pile of buttery crumbs. In its native land, it's known as *torta fregolotti*. You let it stand for a day after baking, then break it into irregular chunks to serve alongside fruit.

> 1 cup blanched almonds, ground
> 2⅔ cups all-purpose flour
> 1 cup sugar
> Pinch of salt
> 1 teaspoon grated lemon peel
> 1 cup (½ lb.) plus 2 tablespoons firm butter or margarine, cut into pieces
> 2 tablespoons lemon juice
> 1 tablespoon brandy or water

In a mixing bowl, stir together almonds, flour, sugar, salt, and lemon peel. With a pastry blender or 2 knives, cut in butter until mixture resembles coarse crumbs. Sprinkle with lemon juice and brandy and mix lightly with a fork until blended. Mixture should be crumbly.

Spread mixture in a greased and flour-dusted 12-inch pizza pan or a 9 by 13-inch baking pan; do not press into pan. Bake in a 350° oven for 50 to 60 minutes or until browned. Let cool completely in pan on a rack.

When cookie is cooled, wrap well (either in or out of pan) and let stand for at least a day. To serve, break into chunks. Store airtight. Makes 2 to 3 dozen pieces.

Cookie Tortes

When you want a dessert with all the charm of a cookie—and a little extra pizzazz—try these special tortes. They start with extra-large round cookies; but when those plain cookies are dressed up with fillings and toppings, cut into wedges, and served with a plate and fork, you'd hardly recognize them. They make a perfect company dessert when your guests are confirmed cookie-lovers.

Chocolate Rum Custard Torte

Rum custard filling (recipe follows)
6 tablespoons solid vegetable shortening
6 tablespoons butter or margarine, softened
1 cup sugar
2 eggs
½ teaspoon vanilla
3 ounces unsweetened chocolate, melted and cooled
2½ cups all-purpose flour
1 teaspoon *each* baking powder and salt
Toasted sliced almonds

Prepare rum custard filling and refrigerate. In large bowl of an electric mixer, beat shortening, butter, and sugar until creamy; beat in eggs, vanilla, and chocolate. In another bowl, stir together flour, baking powder, and salt; gradually add to chocolate mixture, blending thoroughly. Cover tightly with plastic wrap and refrigerate for about 1 hour.

Divide dough into 4 equal portions. Press each portion evenly over bottom of a greased and flour-dusted 9-inch round cake pan with a removable bottom. Bake layers in a 375° oven, 2 at a time, for 15 minutes or until cookies pull away from pan sides. Let cool in pans on racks for 10 minutes; then remove pan sides and slide cookies onto racks. Let cool completely.

To assemble torte, place one cookie layer on a serving plate. Top with a fourth of the filling and spread evenly to within ¼ inch of edge. Repeat layers, ending with filling on top. Invert a large bowl over torte (or place a cake cover over it) and refrigerate for at least 24 hours or for up to 3 days. To serve, sprinkle top with toasted sliced almonds and cut into wedges. Makes 8 to 10 servings.

Rum custard filling. In a 2 to 3-quart pan, stir together ¾ cup **all-purpose flour,** ⅔ cup **sugar,** and ¼ teaspoon **salt.** Gradually stir in 2½ cups **milk** until smooth. Cook over medium heat, stirring constantly, until mixture boils and thickens. Remove from heat.

In a small bowl, lightly beat 3 **egg yolks.** Stir a small amount of hot milk mixture into egg yolks; then slowly return mixture to pan, stirring until well incorporated. Return to heat and cook for 1 more minute. Remove from heat and stir in 1 teaspoon **vanilla** and 2 tablespoons **rum.** Let custard cool, then refrigerate until very thick (3 to 4 hours). Beat ⅓ cup **whipping cream** until stiff; fold into cold custard.

Chocolate Cherry Custard Torte

Prepare **Chocolate Rum Custard Torte** as directed above, but omit rum in custard filling; instead, use 2 tablespoons **kirsch.** Thaw and drain one bag (16 oz.) **frozen pitted red cherries;** cut cherries in half and pat dry with paper towels. Divide cherries into 3 equal portions.

To assemble torte, place one cookie layer on a serving plate. Top with a fourth of the filling and spread evenly to within ¼ inch of edge; then scatter a third of the cherries evenly over filling. Repeat layers, using cherries only on the first three layers and ending with filling on top.

Refrigerate as directed above. Before serving, top with **grated semisweet chocolate** instead of toasted sliced almonds.

Scottish Shortbread

(Pictured on facing page)

Were you to take tea in the highlands, you might be served Scotland's famous shortbread, a butter-rich cookie of delightful simplicity. If you like your shortbread a bit more dressed up, try our ginger variation—or sample Orange-Walnut Shortbread (following), Coconut Shortbread Cookies (page 68), Brown Sugar Shortbread (page 53), or Nutty Whole Wheat Shortbread (page 74).

> 1¼ **cups all-purpose flour**
> 3 **tablespoons cornstarch**
> ¼ **cup sugar**
> ½ **cup (¼ lb.) firm butter, cut into pieces**
> **Sugar**

In a mixing bowl, stir together flour, cornstarch, and the ¼ cup sugar. Rub in butter with your fingers until mixture is very crumbly and no large particles remain. With your hands, gather mixture into a ball; place in an ungreased 8 or 9-inch round baking pan with a removable bottom, or in a 9-inch spring-form pan. Firmly press out dough into an even layer.

With the tines of a fork, make impressions around edge of dough; then prick surface evenly. Bake in a 325° oven for about 40 minutes or until pale golden brown. Remove from oven and, while hot, cut with a sharp knife into 8 to 12 wedges. Sprinkle with about 1 tablespoon sugar. Let cool completely; then remove sides of pan and lift out cookies. Store airtight. Makes 8 to 12.

Ginger Shortbread

Follow directions for **Scottish Shortbread,** but substitute ½ teaspoon **ground ginger** for cornstarch. After rubbing in butter, stir in 2 tablespoons minced **candied ginger.**

Orange-Walnut Shortbread

This orange-flavored shortbread is sprinkled with walnuts and drizzled with an orange glaze while still warm, then cut into tiny squares for bite-size enjoyment with coffee or tea.

> 1¼ **cups all-purpose flour**
> ¼ **cup sugar**
> ⅛ **teaspoon salt**
> 2 **teaspoons grated orange peel**
> ½ **cup (¼ lb.) firm butter, cut into pieces**
> 1 **cup finely chopped walnuts**
> 1 **tablespoon orange juice**
> **Orange glaze (recipe follows)**

In a mixing bowl, stir together flour, sugar, salt, and orange peel. Rub in butter with your fingers until mixture is very crumbly and no large particles remain. Mix in ¾ cup of the walnuts and orange juice. Place mixture in a greased 7 by 11-inch baking pan and press firmly into an even layer.

Bake in a 325° oven for 40 to 45 minutes or until pale golden brown. Meanwhile, prepare orange glaze. Let shortbread cool slightly; then sprinkle with remaining ¼ cup walnuts and drizzle evenly with glaze. Cut into about 1¼-inch squares. Let cool completely in pan on a rack; lift from pan and store airtight. Makes about 4½ dozen.

Orange glaze. In a bowl, stir together ½ cup **powdered sugar,** ½ teaspoon grated **orange peel,** and 2 tablespoons **orange juice** until smooth.

Buttery Cookie Brittle

This delectable confection—part cookie, part candy—is studded with bits of almond brickle.

> ½ **cup (¼ lb.) butter or margarine, softened**
> ¾ **teaspoon vanilla**
> 1 **cup all-purpose flour**
> ½ **cup sugar**
> 1 **package (6 oz.) almond brickle bits**

In large bowl of an electric mixer, beat butter and vanilla until creamy. Blend in flour and sugar, then stir in brickle bits (mixture will be quite crumbly).

Spread mixture evenly over bottom of an ungreased 9 by 13-inch baking pan. Lay a piece of wax paper on top and press firmly to pack crumbs evenly. Discard paper.

Bake in a 375° oven for 15 to 20 minutes or until golden around edges. Let brittle cool in pan on a rack for 10 minutes; then loosen with a wide spatula, turn out onto rack, and let cool completely. Break into pieces. Store airtight for up to 2 days; freeze for longer storage. Makes about 3 dozen 1½ by 2-inch chunks.

Scottish Shortbread *(Recipe on facing page)*

1 Rub butter into flour mixture until very crumbly and no large particles remain.

2 Press dough out firmly into an even layer in an 8 or 9-inch round baking pan with a removable bottom.

3 With tines of a fork, make impressions around edge of dough; then prick surface evenly.

4 Cut baked shortbread into wedges while still warm; for best results, use a ruler as a guide.

Persimmon Bars

After an autumn walk, try serving these soft, spicy bar cookies with glasses of apple cider. Their special flavor comes from bright orange persimmons; a tangy lemon glaze adds extra sparkle.

When preparing the persimmon purée, be sure to use the type of persimmons that become very soft when ripe; you'll recognize them by their pointed tips.

    1 cup persimmon purée (directions follow)
    1 teaspoon baking soda
    1 egg
    1 cup sugar
    ½ cup salad oil
    1 package (8 oz.) pitted dates (about 1½ cups lightly packed), finely snipped
    1¾ cups all-purpose flour
    1 teaspoon *each* salt, ground cinnamon, and ground nutmeg
    ¼ teaspoon ground cloves
    1 cup chopped walnuts or pecans
    Lemon glaze (recipe follows)

Prepare persimmon purée; measure out 1 cup and stir in baking soda. Set aside. In a large bowl, lightly beat egg; then stir in sugar, oil, and dates.

In another bowl, stir together flour, salt, cinnamon, nutmeg, and cloves; add to date mixture alternately with persimmon mixture, stirring just until blended. Stir in walnuts. Spread batter evenly in a lightly greased, flour-dusted 10 by 15-inch rimmed baking pan. Bake in a 350° oven for 25 minutes or until top is lightly browned and a pick inserted in center comes out clean.

Let cool in pan on a rack for 5 minutes. Prepare lemon glaze and spread over cookies. Let cool completely; then cut into 2 by 2½-inch bars. Store covered. Makes 2½ dozen.

Persimmon purée. You'll need fully ripe pointed-tip **persimmons**—pulp should be soft and jellylike. Cut fruits in half and scoop out pulp with a spoon. Discard skin, seeds, and stem. In a blender or food processor, whirl pulp, a portion at a time, until smooth (you'll need 2 or 3 medium-size persimmons for 1 cup purée). For each cup purée, thoroughly stir in 1½ teaspoons **lemon juice.** To store, freeze in 1-cup batches in rigid containers; thaw, covered, at room temperature.

Lemon glaze. In a small bowl, stir together 1 cup **powdered sugar** and 2 tablespoons **lemon juice** until smooth.

Pineapple-Coconut Bars

Transport yourself to the islands with these tropical-tasting bar cookies—they're the next best thing to being on a beach under a palm tree.

    ½ cup (¼ lb.) butter or margarine, softened
    1 cup firmly packed brown sugar
    2 eggs
    ¼ teaspoon almond extract
    ¾ cup all-purpose flour
    ¾ teaspoon baking powder
    ½ teaspoon salt
    ¾ cup flaked coconut
    1 can (8 oz.) crushed pineapple packed in its own juice, drained well

In large bowl of an electric mixer, beat butter and sugar until creamy; beat in eggs and almond extract. In another bowl, stir together flour, baking powder, and salt; gradually add to butter mixture, blending thoroughly. Stir in coconut and pineapple.

Spread mixture evenly in a greased and flour-dusted 9-inch square baking pan. Bake in a 350° oven for 25 to 30 minutes or until top springs back when lightly touched. Let cool in pan on a rack, then cut into 1 by 2¼-inch bars. Store airtight. Makes 3 dozen.

Apple Butter Crumb Bars

Between top and bottom layers of oats and nuts, there's one of dark, flavorful apple butter. These bars can be served as cookies, or cut into bigger pieces and topped with ice cream for a more substantial dessert.

    1½ cups all-purpose flour
    1 teaspoon baking soda
    ½ teaspoon ground cinnamon
    2½ cups quick-cooking rolled oats
    ½ cup chopped nuts
    1 cup firmly packed brown sugar
    1 cup (½ lb.) firm butter or margarine, cut into pieces
    1 jar (16 oz.) apple butter or 1½ cups homemade apple butter

In a mixing bowl, stir together flour, baking soda, cinnamon, oats, nuts, and brown sugar until thoroughly blended. With a pastry blender or 2 knives, cut in butter until mixture is crumbly and no large particles remain.

Spread half the oat mixture evenly over bottom of an ungreased 9 by 13-inch baking pan and press down lightly. Spread apple butter evenly over crumb layer, then sprinkle remaining oat mixture over top; press down lightly.

Bake in a 400° oven for about 25 minutes or until golden brown. Let cool completely in pan on a rack. Cut into bars (about 1½ by 2 inches) or squares (about 2¼ by 2¼ inches). Store covered. Makes 2 to 3 dozen.

Cheesecake Squares

Here's a cookie just for cheesecake lovers. Like cheesecake, the crumb-topped squares are sumptuously creamy—but they're easier to make and more convenient to serve.

    ⅓ cup butter or margarine, softened
    ⅓ cup firmly packed brown sugar
    1 cup all-purpose flour
    ½ cup finely chopped walnuts
    ¼ cup granulated sugar
    1 large package (8 oz.) cream cheese, softened
    1 egg
    ½ teaspoon vanilla
    2 tablespoons milk
    1 tablespoon lemon juice

In large bowl of an electric mixer, beat butter and brown sugar until creamy. With a fork, blend in flour until mixture resembles fine crumbs. Stir in walnuts. Reserve 1 cup crumb mixture for topping; then press remainder firmly and evenly over bottom of a greased 8-inch square baking pan. Bake in a 350° oven for 12 to 15 minutes or until lightly browned.

Meanwhile, in small bowl of mixer, beat granulated sugar and cream cheese until fluffy. Add egg, vanilla, milk, and lemon juice; beat until smooth. Pour cream cheese mixture over baked crust; sprinkle evenly with remaining crumb mixture.

Return to oven and bake for about 20 minutes or until top is lightly browned. Let cool in pan on a rack, then cut into 2-inch squares. Store, covered, in refrigerator. Makes 16.

Dream Bars

(Pictured on page 19)

Of all the cookies that have made a hit over the years, "dream bars" are certainly one of the leaders. Their rich, coconutty filling and buttery crust explain their enduring popularity. Our version of dream bars includes a sweet orange frosting; some cookie connoisseurs wouldn't dream of skipping it, while the purists among us generally prefer our dream bars plain.

    ⅓ cup butter or margarine, softened
    1½ cups firmly packed brown sugar
    1 cup plus 2 tablespoons all-purpose flour
    2 eggs
    1 teaspoon vanilla
    ½ teaspoon salt
    1 teaspoon baking powder
    1½ cups shredded coconut
    1 cup chopped nuts
    Orange butter frosting (optional; recipe follows)

In large bowl of an electric mixer, beat butter and ½ cup of the sugar until creamy. With a fork, blend in 1 cup of the flour until mixture resembles fine crumbs. Press mixture firmly over bottom of a greased 9 by 13-inch baking pan, forming an even layer. Bake in a 375° oven for 10 minutes; let cool in pan on a rack.

Wash and dry mixer bowl. Place eggs in bowl and beat until light and lemon-colored; then gradually beat in remaining 1 cup sugar. Beat in vanilla, remaining 2 tablespoons flour, salt, and baking powder. Stir in coconut and nuts until thoroughly combined.

Pour coconut mixture over baked crust, spreading evenly. Return to oven and bake for 20 minutes or until topping is golden; then let cool in pan on a rack for 10 to 15 minutes. Meanwhile, prepare orange butter frosting, if desired. Cut partially cooled cookies into bars (about 1½ by 3 or 1½ by 2 inches), but do not remove from pan. Spread frosting over cookies and let cool completely in pan on rack. (Don't frost cookies *before* cutting them—if you do, frosting will crack when cookies are cut.) Store covered. Makes 2 to 3 dozen.

Orange butter frosting. In small bowl of an electric mixer, beat 4 tablespoons **butter** or margarine, softened, and 2 cups **powdered sugar** until creamy. Add 1 teaspoon *each* **vanilla** and grated **orange peel.** Beat in enough **orange juice** (about 2 tablespoons) to make a good spreading consistency.

Hand-molded Cookies

When you fashion cookie dough with your hands, you'll be rewarded with a variety of shapes: crescents, balls, pretzels, and more. Hand-molded cookies tend to be fancy, simply because there's so much you can do to the pliable doughs they're made from. They can be rolled in sugar or nuts before baking, filled with jam or jelly, flattened with fork tines in a crisscross pattern—the possibilities are almost endless.

Included in our collection of hand-molded cookies are recipes for special cookies—such as pirouettes and fortune cookies—that are shaped *after* baking, while they're still warm. These take a little extra skill, but once you've practiced on a few, you'll be surprised at how quickly you become proficient.

Hand-molded cookies are often time-consuming to shape, since each morsel of dough must be individually crafted. Most bakers consider them a labor of love, though, and enjoy the shaping process almost as much as the results.

Photo at left shows the variety of cookie shapes you can create with your hands. From top to bottom: Favorite Peanut Butter Cookies (page 32), Italian Fruit Cookies (page 41), Peanut Blossom Cookies (page 32), Pirouettes (page 42), Norwegian Kringle (page 37), Finnish Ribbon Cakes (page 39), Chocolate Chews (page 40), Almond Crescents (page 32), and Chocolate-dipped Hazelnut Bonbons (page 40).

Favorite Peanut Butter Cookies

(Pictured on page 30)

Among the best-known and best-loved of cookies are these traditional treats with crisscrossed tops.

- 1 cup (½ lb.) butter or margarine, softened
- 1 cup peanut butter
- 1 cup firmly packed brown sugar
- 1 cup granulated sugar
- 2 eggs
- 1 teaspoon vanilla
- 3½ cups all-purpose flour
- 1 teaspoon baking soda

In large bowl of an electric mixer, beat butter until creamy. Gradually beat in peanut butter, then brown sugar, then granulated sugar. Beat in eggs, then vanilla.

In another bowl, stir together flour and baking soda; gradually add to butter mixture, blending thoroughly. Roll dough into 1-inch balls and place 2 inches apart on greased baking sheets. Press balls down with a fork, making a crisscross pattern on top of each with fork tines.

Bake in a 375° oven for 10 to 12 minutes or until golden brown. Let cool on baking sheets for about a minute, then transfer to racks and let cool completely. Store airtight. Makes about 7 dozen.

Peanut Blossom Cookies

(Pictured on page 30)

Each of these thick, chewy peanut butter cookies has a chocolate candy kiss on top.

- ½ cup *each* solid vegetable shortening and peanut butter
- ½ cup *each* granulated sugar and firmly packed brown sugar
- 1 egg
- 1 teaspoon vanilla
- 1⅓ cups all-purpose flour
- 1 teaspoon baking soda
- ½ teaspoon salt
- ¼ cup granulated sugar
- 2½ to 3 dozen chocolate candy kisses

In large bowl of an electric mixer, beat shortening, peanut butter, the ½ cup granulated sugar, and brown sugar until creamy; beat in egg and vanilla. In another bowl, stir together flour, baking soda, and salt; gradually add to shortening mixture, blending thoroughly.

Place the ¼ cup granulated sugar in a small bowl. Roll dough into 1-inch balls, then roll in sugar to coat. Place balls 2 inches apart on greased baking sheets.

Bake in a 350° oven for 10 minutes; meanwhile, unwrap chocolate kisses. Remove cookies from oven and quickly top each with a kiss, pressing down until cookie cracks around edges. Return to oven and bake for 3 to 5 more minutes or until cookies are lightly browned and firm to the touch. Transfer to racks and let cool completely. Store airtight. Makes 2½ to 3 dozen.

Almond Crescents

(Pictured on page 30)

A snowy mantle of powdered sugar cloaks these buttery, brandy-spiked nut cookies. Called *kourabiedes*, they're a Greek specialty—but they have close cousins in other cuisines, such as Mexican wedding cakes, Russian teacakes, and Viennese nut crescents.

- ½ cup ground almonds
- 1 cup (½ lb.) unsalted butter or margarine, softened
- 1 egg yolk
- 2 tablespoons powdered sugar
- 1 tablespoon brandy or ½ teaspoon vanilla
- 2 cups all-purpose flour
- ½ teaspoon baking powder
- Whole cloves (optional)
- 1½ to 2 cups powdered sugar

Spread almonds in a shallow pan and toast in a 350° oven for 6 to 8 minutes or until lightly browned. Let cool completely.

In large bowl of an electric mixer, beat butter until creamy. Add egg yolk and the 2 tablespoons powdered sugar, mixing well. Stir in brandy and almonds. In another bowl, stir together flour and baking powder. Gradually add to butter mixture, blending thoroughly.

Pinch off dough in 1-inch balls and roll each into a 3-inch rope. Place ropes about 2 inches apart on ungreased baking sheets; shape into crescents. Insert a whole clove in each crescent, if desired. Bake in a 325° oven for 30 minutes or until very lightly browned. Place baking sheets on racks and let cookies cool for 5 minutes.

Sift about half the 1½ to 2 cups powdered sugar over a sheet of wax paper. Transfer cookies to paper, placing them in a single layer. Sift remaining powdered sugar over cookies to cover. Let stand until cool. Store airtight; remove clove (if used) from each cookie before eating. Makes about 2½ dozen.

Caramel Almond Wafers

German pastry shops offer an impressive array of tempting treats, from fabulous tortes to cookies of every kind. These rich butter wafers come from the city of Bremen; they're crowned with a caramelized almond topping that sinks into the cookies as they bake.

  ½ cup (¼ lb.) butter or margarine, softened
  1 cup sugar
  1 teaspoon vanilla
  1 egg
  1⅔ cups all-purpose flour
  2 teaspoons baking powder
    Sugar
  ⅔ cup whipping cream
  2 teaspoons sugar
  1 cup sliced almonds

In large bowl of an electric mixer, beat butter and the 1 cup sugar until creamy; add vanilla and egg and beat until smooth. In another bowl, stir together flour and baking powder; add to butter mixture, blending thoroughly. Wrap dough in plastic wrap and refrigerate for at least 2 hours or until next day.

Roll dough into 1-inch balls and place 2½ to 3 inches apart on greased baking sheets. Grease bottom of a glass, dip in sugar, and flatten each ball to a thickness of about ¼ inch.

In a 2-quart pan, bring cream and the 2 teaspoons sugar to a boil; continue to boil until reduced by half. Remove from heat and stir in almonds. Spread about 1 teaspoon of the almond mixture on top of each cookie.

Bake in a 325° oven for 12 to 15 minutes or until golden brown. Transfer cookies to racks and let cool. Store airtight. Makes about 4 dozen.

Chinese Almond Cookies

It's hard to imagine a Chinese meal without fortune cookies (page 42)—but these almond-crowned tidbits are actually a more authentic Chinese dessert. Even if you're not serving them with Chinese food, you'll enjoy them as a rich, nutty snack or everyday dessert. If you'd like to vary the recipe, try topping the cookies with pine nuts (used in northern Chinese cooking) or peanuts instead of almonds—or make our sesame-seed variation (below).

  1 cup (½ lb.) lard or solid vegetable shortening
  ½ cup granulated sugar
  ¼ cup firmly packed brown sugar
  1 egg
  1 teaspoon almond extract
  2¼ cups all-purpose flour
  ⅛ teaspoon salt
  1½ teaspoons baking powder
    About 5 dozen whole blanched almonds
  1 egg yolk
  2 tablespoons water

In large bowl of an electric mixer, beat lard with granulated sugar and brown sugar until creamy. Add whole egg and almond extract; beat until well blended. In another bowl, stir together flour, salt, and baking powder; add to creamed mixture, blending thoroughly.

To shape each cookie, roll about 1 tablespoon dough into a ball. Place balls 2 inches apart on ungreased baking sheets, then flatten each slightly to make a 2-inch round. Gently press an almond into center of each round. Place egg yolk and water in a small bowl; beat together lightly with a fork. Brush mixture over top of each cookie with a pastry brush.

Bake in a 350° oven for 10 to 12 minutes or until lightly browned. Transfer to racks and let cool. Store airtight. Makes about 5 dozen.

Chinese Sesame Cookies

Follow directions for **Chinese Almond Cookies,** but substitute about ¼ cup **sesame seeds** for almonds. Press each ball in the palm of your hand to make a 2-inch round. Brush egg mixture on one side of each round, then dip coated side in sesame seeds. Place cookies, seeded side up, on ungreased baking sheets. Bake as for **Chinese Almond Cookies.**

Thumbprint Cookies

(Pictured on facing page)

A sweet "jewel" of jelly sparkles in the center of each of these nutty morsels. It rests in a small indentation made by your thumb—or the tip of a spoon, if you prefer.

  1 cup (½ lb.) butter or margarine, softened
  ½ cup firmly packed brown sugar
  2 eggs
  ½ teaspoon vanilla
  2½ cups all-purpose flour
  ¼ teaspoon salt
  1½ cups finely chopped walnuts
  3 to 4 tablespoons red currant jelly or raspberry jam

In large bowl of an electric mixer, beat butter and sugar until creamy. Separate eggs. Place whites in a small bowl, lightly beat, and set aside; then beat yolks and vanilla into butter mixture. In another bowl, stir together flour and salt. Gradually add to butter mixture, blending thoroughly.

To shape and fill cookies, follow steps 1 through 4 on facing page. Bake in a 375° oven for 12 to 15 minutes or until lightly browned. Let cool on baking sheets for about a minute, then transfer to racks and let cool completely. Store airtight. Makes about 3½ dozen.

Almond Pillows

These crisp brown sugar cookies, each topped with a whole almond, are shaped like little pillows. They're a good choice if you want to bake in quantity, since shaping is quick and easy.

  ½ cup (¼ lb.) butter or margarine, softened
  ½ cup *each* granulated sugar and firmly packed brown sugar
  1 egg
  1 teaspoon vanilla
  2 cups all-purpose flour
  ½ teaspoon salt
  1 teaspoon baking powder
  ¾ teaspoon ground cardamom
  1 teaspoon ground cinnamon
  5 dozen whole blanched almonds

In large bowl of an electric mixer, beat butter, granulated sugar, and brown sugar until creamy. Add egg and vanilla and beat until combined.

In another bowl, stir together flour, salt, baking powder, cardamom, and cinnamon; gradually add to butter mixture, blending thoroughly. Turn mixture out onto a lightly floured board and divide into 4 equal portions.

Roll each portion into a 15-inch rope. Cut each rope into 1-inch pieces and gently press an almond into each piece. Place cookies 2 inches apart on ungreased baking sheets. Bake in a 350° oven for 15 minutes or until lightly browned. Let cool on baking sheets for about a minute, then transfer to racks and let cool completely. Store airtight. Makes 5 dozen.

Pine Nut Crescents

These generously proportioned crescents, studded with pine nuts, are typical of cookies sold in the *pâtisseries* of Provence, France. A honey glaze subtly complements the faintly resinous flavor of the nuts; a touch of orange flower water adds a special, sweet fragrance. (Orange flower water is a concentrated, nonalcoholic flavoring that's available at most liquor stores.)

  1 cup (½ lb.) butter or margarine, softened
  ⅔ cup firmly packed brown sugar
  3 egg yolks
  1 teaspoon *each* orange flower water and grated orange peel
  ½ teaspoon vanilla
  2¾ cups all-purpose flour
    About ½ cup pine nuts
  3 tablespoons honey

In large bowl of an electric mixer, beat butter and sugar until creamy. Beat in egg yolks, one at a time; beat in orange flower water, orange peel, and vanilla. Add flour and stir until well blended.

To make each cookie, roll about 1 tablespoon dough between lightly floured hands into a 2½-inch rope. Place ropes about 2 inches apart on greased baking sheets; shape into crescents. Scatter pine nuts over cookies and press in firmly. Heat honey over low heat until it liquefies completely, then brush liberally over cookies.

Bake in a 325° oven for 15 to 20 minutes or until golden. Transfer to racks and let cool. Store airtight. Makes about 3½ dozen.

Thumbprint Cookies (*Recipe on facing page*)

1 With your hands, roll dough into balls about 1 inch in diameter.

2 Dip each ball in egg whites, then roll in finely chopped walnuts to coat. Place on greased baking sheets, spacing 1 inch apart.

3 With your thumb or the tip of a spoon, make an indentation in the center of each ball.

4 Neatly fill each indentation with about ¼ teaspoon red currant jelly or raspberry jam.

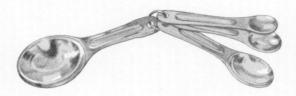

Cookie Sculpture

Making these whimsical cookies is child's play—you just press, pinch, mold, cut, or roll dough into whatever shapes you like. It's an engrossing family project for a rainy day, or a good party activity for kids—and best of all, it results in an assortment of edible sculptures for enjoying at home or giving away. To package the cookies as gifts, wrap in clear or colored cellophane and tape shut, or heat-seal in plastic wrap as directed on page 5.

Honey-Lemon Sculpture Cookies

  5½ **cups all-purpose flour**
   3 **teaspoons baking soda**
  1¾ **cups sugar**
   ¼ **teaspoon salt**
   ¼ **cup honey**
   2 **teaspoons vanilla**
   3 **teaspoons grated lemon or orange peel**
   1 **cup (½ lb.) butter or margarine, melted**
   ½ **cup boiling water**
   1 **egg, lightly beaten**

In a large bowl, combine flour and baking soda; set aside. In another large bowl, combine sugar, salt, honey, vanilla, and lemon peel; add butter and water and beat until sugar is dissolved. Gradually stir in flour mixture to form a stiff dough.

Use dough immediately, or cover tightly with plastic wrap and refrigerate for up to 2 days. For longer storage, wrap in plastic wrap and freeze. Bring dough to room temperature before shaping (let frozen dough thaw in its wrapping).

To shape dough, use any of the following techniques—or devise your own methods.

Cookie-cutter composites. On a floured board, roll out dough to a thickness of ⅛ to ¼ inch. Cut with floured cookie cutters. Arrange cutouts on greased baking sheets, combining shapes and overlapping edges to build decorative images. Be sure completed cookies are spaced at least 1 inch apart.

Cutouts with appliqués. Roll dough out on a floured board to a thickness of ⅛ to ¼ inch (for large cookies, roll directly on a greased unrimmed baking sheet). Cut out shapes with floured cutters—or design paper patterns, place them on dough, and cut around edges with a sharp knife. Space cookies at least 1 inch apart on a greased baking sheet.

To make appliqués, shape small pieces of dough into dabs, dots, narrow ropes, or whatever other forms you like, and press these lightly onto the cookie base. For best results, don't build up cookies thicker than ¾ inch.

Rolled ropes. Roll small pieces of dough on a floured board or between your hands to form even ropes ¼ to ½ inch thick. Make these into letters or numbers, or appliqué onto other dough forms to make arms or legs. Place cookies at least 1 inch apart on greased baking sheets.

Freeform sculptures. Pinch or press dough to make shapes, or roll it out and cut it freehand with a sharp knife. Place cookies at least 1 inch apart on greased baking sheets.

To bake cookies, brush with beaten egg. Bake in a 300° oven for 20 to 30 minutes or until golden at edges. Let cool on baking sheets for at least 10 minutes; then transfer to racks and let cool completely.

Wrap cookies airtight and store at room temperature for up to 2 weeks, or freeze for longer storage. Makes 1½ to 2 dozen large cookies.

Snickerdoodles

Delicately crisp outside, soft and cakelike inside, these old-fashioned cookies with their cinnamon-sugar coating make dainty nibbling with a cup of tea.

    1 cup (½ lb.) butter or margarine, softened
1⅓ cups sugar
    2 eggs
    1 teaspoon vanilla
    3 cups all-purpose flour
    1 teaspoon *each* baking soda and cream of tartar
    ¼ teaspoon salt
    2 teaspoons ground cinnamon
    3 tablespoons sugar

In large bowl of an electric mixer, beat butter and the 1⅓ cups sugar until creamy. Beat in eggs and vanilla. In another bowl, stir together flour, baking soda, cream of tartar, and salt; gradually add to butter mixture, blending thoroughly.

In a small bowl, combine cinnamon and the 3 tablespoons sugar. Roll dough into 1-inch balls, then roll in cinnamon-sugar mixture to coat. Place at least 2 inches apart on greased baking sheets. Bake in a 375° oven for about 12 minutes or until lightly browned. Let cool on baking sheets for about a minute, then transfer to racks and let cool completely. Store airtight. Makes about 4½ dozen.

Norwegian Kringle

(Pictured on page 30)

Hard-cooked egg yolks lend extra richness to the dough for *kringle,* Norway's pretzel-shaped butter cookies.

    1 cup (½ lb.) butter, softened
    1 cup sugar
    1 egg
    2 hard-cooked egg yolks, finely mashed
    1 teaspoon vanilla
    3 cups all-purpose flour
    ¼ teaspoon salt
    1 egg white, lightly beaten
       Granulated sugar or coarsely crushed sugar cubes

In large bowl of an electric mixer, beat butter and the 1 cup sugar until creamy; beat in egg, egg yolks, and vanilla until well combined. In another bowl, stir together flour and salt; gradually add to butter mixture, blending thoroughly. Wrap dough in plastic wrap and refrigerate for at least 1 hour or until next day.

Pinch off 1-inch balls of dough and roll each into a 6-inch-long strand. Form each strand into a pretzel shape on greased baking sheets, spacing pretzels about an inch apart. Using a pastry brush, brush cookies with egg white; then sprinkle with sugar.

Bake in a 350° oven for 12 to 15 minutes or until pale golden brown. Transfer to racks and let cool completely. Store airtight. Makes about 4 dozen.

Orange Coconut Crisps

The coconut is native to the tropics, where it's used in hundreds of different ways. Cooks in cooler climates have developed lots of delectable coconut recipes, too—such as these crisp cookies. They combine coconut with a subtle touch of orange for extra-tempting flavor.

    1 cup (½ lb.) butter or margarine, softened
    1 cup sugar
    1 egg
    1 teaspoon *each* grated orange peel and vanilla
1½ cups all-purpose flour
    1 cup cornstarch
    1 teaspoon baking powder
    ¼ teaspoon salt
1⅓ cups flaked or shredded coconut

In large bowl of an electric mixer, beat butter and sugar until creamy; beat in egg, orange peel, and vanilla. In another bowl, stir together flour, cornstarch, baking powder, and salt. Gradually add to butter mixture, blending thoroughly. Add coconut and mix until well combined. Cover dough tightly with plastic wrap and refrigerate for about 2 hours.

Roll dough into 1 to 1¼-inch balls and arrange about 2 inches apart on greased baking sheets. With tines of a fork, flatten each ball to a thickness of about ¼ inch. Bake in a 375° oven for 8 to 10 minutes or until lightly browned. Let cool for about a minute on baking sheets, then transfer to racks and let cool completely. Store airtight. Makes about 4 dozen.

Koulourakia *(Recipe on facing page)*

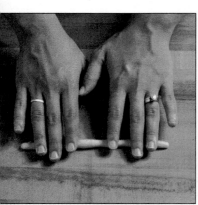

1 Pinch off balls of dough about 1 inch in diameter, then roll each into a 7-inch strand.

2 Fold strand in half lengthwise. With one end in each hand, twist ends of folded strand in opposite directions.

3 Brush twists lightly with egg yolk mixture. This helps sesame seeds stick and gives finished cookies a rich golden color.

4 Sprinkle cookies with sesame seeds before baking; you'll need 2 to 3 tablespoons.

Koulourakia

(Pictured on facing page)

At Eastertime in Greece, these sesame-topped cookies are enjoyed by the dozen. Like shortbread, they're crunchy, buttery, and not too sweet.

- ½ cup (¼ lb.) butter or margarine, softened
- ½ cup sugar
- 3 egg yolks
- ¼ cup half-and-half (light cream)
- 2¼ cups all-purpose flour
- 1 teaspoon baking powder
- ¼ teaspoon salt
- 2 to 3 tablespoons sesame seeds

In large bowl of an electric mixer, beat butter and sugar until creamy. Beat in 2 of the egg yolks, one at a time. Mix in 3 tablespoons of the half-and-half. In another bowl, stir together flour, baking powder, and salt; gradually add to butter mixture, blending thoroughly.

To shape cookies, pinch off 1-inch balls of dough; roll each into a 7-inch strand. Bring ends together and twist (see photo 2 on facing page) or form into a pretzel shape. Place slightly apart on greased baking sheets. Beat remaining egg yolk with remaining 1 tablespoon half-and-half; brush lightly over cookies and sprinkle with sesame seeds. Bake in a 350° oven for about 15 minutes or until golden. Transfer to racks and let cool completely. Store airtight. Makes about 2½ dozen.

White Chocolate Chip Cookies

This variation on a favorite American cookie uses white chocolate instead of dark. You'll find white chocolate in candy stores and gourmet shops.

- 1 cup (½ lb.) butter or margarine, softened
- 1½ cups sugar
- 2 teaspoons baking soda
- 1 egg
- 1 cup all-purpose flour
- 2 cups quick-cooking rolled oats
- 6 ounces (1¼ cups) white chocolate, coarsely chopped

In large bowl of an electric mixer, beat butter, sugar, and baking soda until creamy; beat in egg. Gradually add flour and oats, blending thoroughly. Stir in chocolate.

Roll dough into ¾-inch balls and place 2 inches apart on ungreased baking sheets. Bake in a 350° oven for 10 to 12 minutes or until light golden. Let cool on baking sheets until firm to the touch, then transfer to racks and let cool completely. Store airtight for up to 3 days. Makes about 5 dozen.

Finnish Ribbon Cakes

(Pictured on page 30)

For holiday (or everyday) entertaining, offer a platter of assorted Scandinavian cookies: Swedish Spritz (page 55), Norwegian Kringle (page 37), and these fancy Finnish morsels.

- 1 cup (½ lb.) butter or margarine, softened
- ½ cup sugar
- 1 egg yolk
- 1 teaspoon vanilla
- ½ teaspoon grated lemon peel
- 2½ cups all-purpose flour
- ¼ teaspoon salt
- About 6 tablespoons raspberry or apricot jam
- ½ cup powdered sugar mixed with 1 tablespoon water

In large bowl of an electric mixer, beat butter and sugar until creamy; beat in egg yolk, vanilla, and lemon peel. In another bowl, stir together flour and salt. Gradually add to butter mixture, blending thoroughly.

Shape dough into ropes about ¾ inch in diameter and as long as your baking sheets; place them about 2 inches apart on ungreased baking sheets. With the side of your little finger, press a long groove down the center of each rope (don't press all the way down to baking sheets). Bake cookies in a 375° oven for 10 minutes.

Remove cookies from oven and spoon jam into the grooves. Return to oven for 5 to 10 minutes or until cookies are firm to touch and light golden brown. While cookies are hot, drizzle them with powdered sugar mixture (or spread mixture along sides of cookies). Then cut at a 45° angle into 1-inch lengths. Let cool briefly on baking sheets; transfer to racks and let cool completely. Store airtight. Makes about 4 dozen.

Old-fashioned Molasses Chews

How to glorify a glass of milk? Enjoy it with a plateful of these big, spicy molasses cookies. Their tops are sugary and crinkled, their interiors moist and chewy.

> ¾ cup salad oil
> ¼ cup dark molasses
> 1¼ cups sugar
> 2 eggs
> 2¾ cups all-purpose flour
> 1½ teaspoons baking soda
> 1 teaspoon *each* ground cinnamon and ginger
> ¼ teaspoon ground cloves

In a large bowl, stir together oil, molasses, and 1 cup of the sugar. Add eggs and beat until smooth. In another bowl, stir together flour, baking soda, cinnamon, ginger, and cloves; gradually add to molasses mixture, beating until well combined. Cover tightly with plastic wrap and refrigerate for at least 1 hour or until next day.

Place remaining ¼ cup sugar in a small bowl. Roll dough into 1½-inch balls, then roll in sugar to coat. Place 3 inches apart on greased baking sheets. Bake in a 350° oven for 10 to 12 minutes or until lightly browned. Transfer to racks and let cool completely. Store airtight. Makes about 2½ dozen.

Chocolate Chews

(Pictured on page 30)

Satisfying a chocolate lover is never easy, but these dark, sugary cookies can help. Their crinkly tops and chewy texture will remind you of Old-fashioned Molasses Chews (above).

> 1 package (6 oz.) semisweet chocolate chips
> ½ cup (¼ lb.) butter or margarine, softened
> 1¼ cups sugar
> 2 eggs
> 2 cups all-purpose flour
> ¼ teaspoon salt
> ½ teaspoon *each* baking powder and baking soda

In top of a double boiler over simmering water or in a small pan over lowest possible heat, stir chocolate chips just until melted; set aside. In large bowl of an electric mixer, beat butter and 1 cup of the sugar until creamy; beat in eggs and melted chocolate. In another bowl, stir together flour, salt, baking powder, and baking soda; gradually add to butter mixture, blending thoroughly.

Place remaining ¼ cup sugar in a small bowl. Roll dough into 1-inch balls and roll in sugar to coat; place at least 2 inches apart on greased baking sheets. Bake in a 350° oven for 12 to 14 minutes or until tops appear dry. Let cool on baking sheets for about a minute, then transfer to racks and let cool completely. Store airtight. Makes about 3½ dozen.

Chocolate-dipped Hazelnut Bonbons

(Pictured on page 30)

Add variety to a cookie tray with these chewy, no-bake bonbons made from toasted hazelnuts. If you prefer, you can use whole blanched almonds in place of hazelnuts; you'll need 3 cups.

> 1 pound (3½ cups) hazelnuts (filberts), whole or in large pieces
> 2 cups powdered sugar
> 5 to 6 tablespoons egg whites (whites of about 3 large eggs)
> About 6 ounces semisweet chocolate chips

Spread hazelnuts in a 10 by 15-inch rimmed baking pan. Bake in a 350° oven for 10 to 15 minutes or until pale golden beneath skins, shaking pan occasionally. (If using almonds, toast for 8 to 10 minutes.) Pour nuts into a dishcloth and fold cloth to enclose; rub briskly to remove as much of skins as possible (see photo on page 75; omit this step if using almonds). Lift nuts from cloth and let cool.

Coarsely chop nuts. In a food processor or blender, finely grind nuts, about ⅓ at a time, until mealy.

Return all nuts to food processor and add sugar and 5 tablespoons egg whites. Process until a paste forms, adding more egg whites if needed. (Or mix ground nuts with egg whites and sugar with a heavy-duty mixer on low speed; or knead by hand until mixture sticks together.) If mixture is too soft to shape, wrap in plastic wrap and refrigerate for about 1 hour.

Roll nut paste into 1-inch balls; set 1 inch apart on wax-paper-lined rimmed baking pans, pressing balls down to flatten bottoms slightly.

In top of a double boiler over simmering water or in a small pan over lowest possible heat, stir chocolate chips just until melted. Dip each ball (by hand) into chocolate to cover top half; return to paper-lined pan, chocolate side up. Refrigerate, uncovered, until chocolate is set (about 30 minutes). Serve at once, or cover and refrigerate for up to 1 week; let stand at room temperature for about 15 minutes before serving. Makes 3 to 4 dozen.

Italian Nut Cookies

An Italian inclination is to dunk a cookie into wine or coffee before eating it, so it comes as no surprise that Italian cookies are often firm in texture. These rusk-type cookies are studded with nuts and flavored with anise; you bake them twice, to a toasty crunchiness.

    2 **cups sugar**
    1 **cup (½ lb.) butter or margarine, melted**
  ¼ **cup anise seeds**
  ¼ **cup anisette or other anise-flavored liqueur**
    3 **tablespoons whiskey, or 2 teaspoons vanilla and 2 tablespoons water**
    6 **eggs**
5½ **cups all-purpose flour**
    3 **teaspoons baking powder**
    2 **cups coarsely chopped almonds or walnuts**

In a large bowl, stir together sugar, butter, anise seeds, anisette, and whiskey. Beat in eggs. In another bowl, stir together flour and baking powder; gradually add to sugar mixture, blending thoroughly. Mix in almonds. Cover tightly with plastic wrap and refrigerate for 2 to 3 hours.

Directly on greased baking sheets, shape dough with your hands to form flat loaves about ½ inch thick, 2 inches wide, and as long as baking sheets. Place loaves parallel and 4 inches apart. Bake in a 375° oven for 20 minutes or until lightly browned.

Remove loaves from oven and let cool on baking sheets until you can touch them; then cut diagonally into ½ to ¾-inch-thick slices. Place slices close together, cut sides down, on baking sheets; bake in 375° oven for 15 more minutes or until lightly toasted. Transfer to racks to cool. Store airtight. Makes about 9 dozen.

Italian Fruit Cookies

(Pictured on page 30)

Follow directions for **Italian Nut Cookies,** but in place of almonds use 1½ cups diced **mixed candied fruit** and ½ cup **pine nuts** or slivered almonds. Second baking will take 12 to 15 minutes.

German Oatmeal Lace Cookies

Fragile, snowflake prettiness isn't usually expected of oatmeal cookies, but these lacy German treats have just that. When warm, they're flexible enough to be curved, rolled, folded, or bent into various shapes—or you can just leave them flat. The cooled cookies are crisp and brittle, almost like candy.

  ⅔ **cup quick-cooking rolled oats**
  ¼ **cup all-purpose flour**
  ¼ **teaspoon** *each* **salt, ground cloves, and ground ginger**
  ½ **cup sugar**
  ½ **cup (¼ lb.) butter or margarine**
    2 **tablespoons whipping cream**

In a small pan, combine all ingredients. Cook over medium heat, stirring, until mixture begins to bubble. Remove from heat and stir well. Drop dough, 1 level teaspoonful at a time, onto lightly greased baking sheets (they must be flat, not warped), allowing 3 or 4 cookies per sheet.

Bake in a 375° oven for 5 to 7 minutes or until evenly browned (bake only one sheet at a time if you wish to shape cookies; they cool quickly). Place baking sheet on a rack and let cookies cool until firm enough to lift from pan with a spatula but still soft enough to shape—less than a minute. (For flat cookies, leave cookies on baking sheets until firm, then transfer to racks and let cool completely.)

To shape cookies, wrap them around metal pastry tubes or cones that are at least ½ inch in diameter (or make your own forms from several thicknesses of foil). Let cool on racks, then remove forms. Or drape cookies over horizontally suspended wooden spoon handles or a broomstick and let stand until completely cool. If cookies become too stiff to shape, you can restore their flexibility by returning them briefly to the oven. Store airtight. Makes 3 to 4 dozen.

Fortune Cookies

(Pictured on facing page)

Fortune cookies: A traditional sweet made from an ancient Chinese recipe? Hardly. Fortune cookies aren't really Chinese at all—they're the innovation of an enterprising Los Angeles baker in the 1920s. But they taste good, and they're always popular with Chinese food or as snacks.

Making fortune cookies at home is easy once you get the hang of it. You bake the batter in flat circles, and then shape each cookie while it's hot, enclosing a fortune inside. Wear trim-fitting cotton gloves to protect your hands, and work quickly—each cookie must be formed within 15 seconds. After that, it begins to harden.

For the fortunes, consult books of poetry or proverbs, or rely on your own wit. Original messages are a good way to provide entertainment, and fate has a curious way of matching people to appropriate fortunes.

> 1 **cup all-purpose flour**
> 2 **tablespoons cornstarch**
> ½ **cup sugar**
> ½ **teaspoon salt**
> ½ **cup salad oil**
> ½ **cup egg whites (whites of about 4 large eggs)**
> 1 **tablespoon water**
> 2 **teaspoons vanilla**

Type or print fortunes, allowing a ½ by 3-inch area of paper for each. Then cut paper into strips, separating individual fortunes; place near oven. Also have ready a saucepan or straight-sided bowl for shaping and a muffin pan for cooling the cookies. In a bowl, stir together flour, cornstarch, sugar, and salt. Add oil and egg whites and beat until smooth; beat in water and vanilla.

Drop batter by level tablespoonfuls on a well-greased baking sheet and spread out evenly with the back of a spoon into 4-inch circles. (Bake only 1 or 2 cookies per sheet at first, then increase to 4 per sheet as your shaping speed improves.) Bake in a 300° oven for about 14 minutes or until light golden brown; if underbaked, cookies will tear during shaping.

With a wide spatula, remove one cookie at a time from oven. Working quickly, follow steps 1 through 4 on facing page. If cookie hardens too fast, you can restore its flexibility by returning it to the oven for about a minute. Repeat for remaining batter, using a cold, well-greased baking sheet for each batch. Store airtight. Makes about 2½ dozen.

Giant Fortune Cookies

Type or print fortunes, allowing a 1 by 3-inch area of paper for each. Cut paper into strips, separating individual fortunes. Prepare batter as directed for **Fortune Cookies**.

Bake 1 cookie at a time: drop a level 1/3 cup of batter onto a greased baking sheet and spread evenly into a 10-inch circle. Bake as directed. Immediately remove cookie from baking sheet and shape as for **Fortune Cookies** (see steps 1 through 4 at right), but crease cookie by hand and hold it for a minute or two to maintain its shape as it cools (giant cookies are too big to crease over a pan edge or cool in a muffin pan). Repeat until all batter is used. Makes 6.

Pirouettes

(Pictured on page 30)

These delicate, lemon-scented cookies are rolled into graceful scrolls while still warm. They make an elegant addition to a platter of teatime fancies; you might also try serving them as a crisp and pretty accompaniment to chocolate mousse or fruit sorbet.

> 6 **tablespoons butter or margarine, softened**
> 1 **cup powdered sugar**
> ⅔ **cup all-purpose flour**
> ½ **teaspoon grated lemon peel**
> 1 **teaspoon vanilla**
> 4 **egg whites**

In small bowl of an electric mixer, beat butter and sugar until creamy. Gradually add flour and lemon peel and beat until well combined; then add vanilla and egg whites and beat until batter is smooth.

Bake cookies 4 at a time. First, drop four 1½-teaspoon portions well apart on a well-greased baking sheet; then spread each thinly with a spatula or knife to make an oblong about 3 by 4 inches. Bake in a 425° oven for 3 minutes or until edges begin to brown.

Remove from oven and quickly roll each cookie lengthwise around a wooden spoon handle or chopstick to form a scroll. (If your fingers are sensitive to heat, wear trim-fitting cotton gloves to protect them.) Slide cookie off spoon handle and let cool on a rack. Repeat baking and rolling until all batter is used. Store airtight. Makes about 3 dozen.

will take a long journey

Fortune Cookies *(Recipe on facing page)*

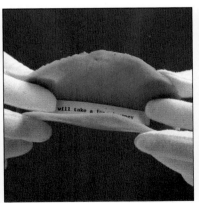

1 Reach into oven with a wide spatula, remove one cookie, and flip it over into gloved hand.

2 Hold prepared fortune in center of cookie while you fold it in half; work quickly.

3 Grasp ends of cookie and draw gently down over the edge of a pan or bowl to crease.

4 To ensure that cookies hold their shape as they finish cooling, place them, ends down, in muffin pans.

Cookies & Ice Cream

Cookies and ice cream go well together, offering appealing contrasts in flavor and texture. You can always enjoy this compatible combination simply by serving a few crisp wafers alongside a dish of ice cream; but when you're in the mood for something more elaborate, try one of the following presentations.

Our first cookies-and-cream specialty is a chocolate-covered ice cream sandwich made with chewy homemade oatmeal cookies and your favorite ice cream. The second is a crisp, lacy cookie "basket" that holds ice cream and your choice of fresh fruit for a special summer dessert. And the third is a homemade ice cream cone, made from an almond-flavored cookie batter that bakes in a waffle iron. True devotees of cookies and ice cream will want to try all three.

Ice Cream Sandwiches

  ¾ **cup solid vegetable shortening**
  1 **cup firmly packed brown sugar**
  ½ **cup granulated sugar**
  1 **egg**
  ¼ **cup water**
  1 **teaspoon vanilla**
  1 **cup all-purpose flour**
  1 **teaspoon salt**
  ½ **teaspoon baking soda**
  3 **cups rolled oats**
  1 **cup chopped nuts**
  ½ **gallon brick-packed ice cream (vanilla, coffee, peppermint, or other)**
  3 **packages (6 oz. each) plain or mint-flavored semisweet chocolate chips**
  5 **tablespoons solid vegetable shortening**

In large bowl of an electric mixer, beat together the ¾ cup shortening, brown sugar, and granu-lated sugar until creamy. Beat in egg, water, and vanilla until well combined. In another bowl, stir together flour, salt, and baking soda; gradually add to sugar mixture, blending thoroughly. Stir in oats and nuts.

Divide batter between 2 greased 10 by 15-inch rimmed baking pans. Spread batter evenly over bottom of one pan; bake in a 350° oven for 12 minutes or until surface is just dry (don't overbake, or cookies won't be chewy). While first pan bakes, spread batter evenly over bottom of second pan.

Remove first pan from oven. Using a sharp knife and a ruler, immediately cut into 16 rectangles, each 2½ by 3¾ inches. Remove cookies from pan while warm; let cool completely on racks. Bake the second pan while cutting cookies from the first; cut into 16 more rectangles, transfer to racks, and let cool completely before assembling sandwiches.

To assemble sandwiches: Cut 8 crosswise slices, each ½ to ¾ inch thick, from brick of ice cream; cut each slice in half. Sandwich each ice cream slice between 2 cookies. Place on a baking sheet and freeze, uncovered, until firm (about 4 hours).

To coat sandwiches: Place chocolate chips in top of a double boiler with the 5 tablespoons shortening. Place over simmering water; stir until melted and smooth (temperature should be 100°F to 110°F). If overheated, chocolate becomes too thick; to thin it, remove from heat and stir a few times until it cools. To reheat, place over simmering water and stir until melted and smooth again.

Coat sandwiches a few at a time. Take from freezer; trim off any uneven cookie edges, if desired. With a new paintbrush or a soft pastry brush, coat ice cream edges with chocolate, then place sandwiches on a baking sheet and coat tops. Freeze, uncovered, until firm (about 45 minutes).

Reheat chocolate. Turn sandwiches over and coat remaining side. Freeze again, uncovered, until firm (about 45 minutes). Wrap each sandwich in foil and store in freezer. Makes 16.

Cookie Baskets

- 4 tablespoons butter or margarine
- ¼ cup *each* firmly packed brown sugar and light corn syrup
- 3½ tablespoons all-purpose flour
- ½ cup finely chopped nuts
- 1 teaspoon vanilla
  Vanilla or nut ice cream
- 1½ to 2 cups fresh fruit, cut into bite-size pieces if necessary (optional)

In a 1 to 2-quart pan, melt butter over low heat. Add sugar and corn syrup. Increase heat to high; bring mixture to a boil, stirring constantly. Remove from heat, add flour and nuts, and stir until blended. Stir in vanilla.

Grease and flour-dust 2 baking sheets (they must be flat, not warped). For each cookie, use a 2 to 3-tablespoon portion of batter; drop portions about 8 inches apart on sheets. (Depending on baking sheet size and cookie size, you'll only be able to bake 1 or 2 cookies on each sheet.) If the batter has cooled and does not flow easily, evenly press or spread it out to a 3 to 4-inch circle.

Bake in a 325° oven for about 12 minutes or until a rich golden brown all over. (You can bake 2 sheets of cookies at a time, staggering sheets in oven and switching their positions halfway through baking to ensure even browning.) Place baking sheets on racks and let cool until cookie edges are just firm enough to lift (about 1 minute). Cookie should be hot, flexible, and somewhat stretchy, but cooled enough to be moved without pulling apart.

Loosen edges with a wide spatula, then slide spatula under entire cookie to remove. Turn cookie over and drape over an inverted glass that measures about 2 inches across the bottom. With your hand, gently cup cookie around the glass; make bottom flat and flare out cookie at sides.

If cookies become too firm to shape, return to oven for a few minutes or until pliable.

Let shaped cookies cool until firm (about 2 minutes). Gently remove from glasses. Repeat, using remaining batter and greasing and reflouring baking sheets each time.

Use baskets at once. Or store airtight in rigid containers at room temperature for up to 1 week; or freeze for longer storage. To serve, place a small scoop of ice cream in each basket and top with fruit, if desired. Break off pieces of cookie to eat along with ice cream and fruit. Makes 4 to 6.

Cookie Cones

- 3 eggs
- ⅔ cup sugar
- ⅔ cup butter or margarine, melted
- 2 teaspoons vanilla
- 1 teaspoon almond extract
- 1 cup all-purpose flour

In a medium-size bowl, beat together eggs, sugar, butter, vanilla, and almond extract. Add flour and stir until smoothly blended. Place flat griddle plates on an electric waffle iron and preheat to medium-hot.

Cone forms should be about 7 inches long, with a 2½-inch top opening. Use purchased metal cream horn forms or purchased pointed sugar cones wrapped with foil; or make your own forms out of lightweight cardboard. You'll need only 1 or 2 forms.

For each 5-inch cone (maximum size for most rectangular griddles), use 1½ tablespoons of batter; for a 7 to 8-inch cone, use 3 to 4 tablespoons. Pour batter onto center of hot griddle (lightly grease griddle for first few cookies, if necessary); close tightly to flatten. Let bake until golden brown (1½ to 2 minutes).

Quickly lift off cookie with a fork or spatula and place on a flat surface. Immediately wrap cookie around cone form, holding it firmly at tip to make a sharp point. (If your fingers are sensitive to heat, wear trim-fitting cotton gloves.) Place cookie on a rack, seam side down, and let cool until firm (about 2 minutes). Remove cone form to use again.

If made ahead, carefully stack and store airtight in rigid containers for up to 1 week; freeze for longer storage. Makes about 1½ dozen small cones, about 9 large cones.

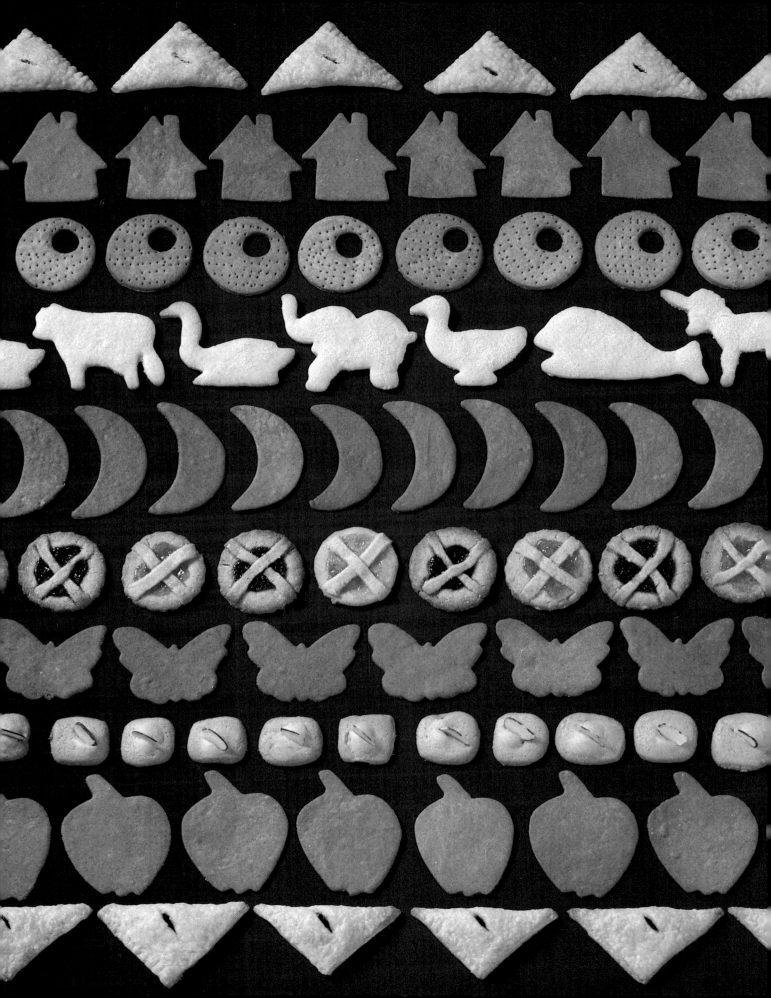

Cut-out & Specialty Cookies

These cookies get their distinct, well-defined shapes from special tools. Cut-out cookies, as most bakers know, are made by rolling out the dough with a rolling pin, then cutting it into plain or fancy shapes with cookie cutters. You can also use a knife as a cutting tool; or use a pastry wheel to obtain a pretty, fluted edge (see Crisp-fried Knots, page 50). Once the cookies are cut, they may be filled in various ways to produce turnovers, horns, and other fancy creations.

Another type of cookie shaped with special equipment is the pressed cookie, which is made by forcing a soft dough through a cookie press or pastry bag to yield such treats as Spritz (page 55) and Ladyfingers (page 56). We also include a half-dozen recipes for cookie-iron cookies, which get their patterned surfaces from gadgets resembling waffle irons; for examples, see pages 58 to 61.

Photo at left presents a procession of cut-out cookies on parade. From top to bottom: Flaky Fruit Turnovers (page 56); Swedish Ginger Thins (page 49); Finnish Rye Cookies (page 48); Sugar Cookies (page 50); Swedish Ginger Thins; Viennese Jam Rounds (page 58); Swedish Ginger Thins; Almond Ravioli Cookies (page 57); Swedish Ginger Thins; and Flaky Fruit Turnovers.

Cut-out Cookies

For these cookies, you'll need a rolling pin and a flat surface. How the dough is cut varies from recipe to recipe; while most use cookie cutters, a few call for knives or pastry wheels. Our collection of cut-out cookies includes a variety of types—some plain, some sugared or frosted, and one that's colorfully painted with water-color brushes and food color "paints."

Anise Cookies

The secret of these cookies' flavor is anise sugar: plain granulated sugar that has been mixed with anise seeds, then allowed to stand for a day. When you make the cookies, you can add the seeds to the dough along with the sugar, or sift them out first for a subtler flavor.

- ¾ cup sugar
- 2 teaspoons anise seeds
- 1 cup (½ lb.) butter or margarine, softened
- 1 egg
- 2 tablespoons brandy or 1 tablespoon *each* lemon juice and water
- 3 cups all-purpose flour
- 1 teaspoon baking powder
- ½ teaspoon salt
- ½ teaspoon ground cinnamon

Combine sugar and anise seeds; cover tightly and let stand for about 24 hours. Sift out and discard seeds, if desired.

In large bowl of an electric mixer, beat butter and ½ cup of the anise sugar until creamy. Beat in egg and brandy. In another bowl, stir together flour, baking powder, salt, and cinnamon; gradually add to butter mixture, blending thoroughly. Gather dough into a ball, wrap tightly in plastic wrap, and refrigerate until firm (about 1 hour) or for up to 3 days.

Roll out dough on a lightly floured board to a thickness of ⅛ inch. Cut out with cookie cutters (about 2½ inches in diameter) and place 1 inch apart on lightly greased baking sheets. Sift and discard seeds from remaining ¼ cup anise sugar (if you haven't already done so) and sprinkle sugar evenly over cookies.

Bake in a 350° oven for about 12 minutes or until golden brown. Transfer to racks and let cool. Store airtight. Makes about 5 dozen.

Nutmeg Crisps

Made from a buttermilk dough and flavored with ground nutmeg, these simple cookies go well with tea or coffee. For extra-fresh nutmeg flavor, try buying whole nutmeg and grating it yourself.

- 1 cup (½ lb.) butter or margarine, softened
- 1 cup sugar
- 1 egg
- 3½ cups all-purpose flour
- ⅛ teaspoon salt
- 1 teaspoon *each* ground nutmeg and baking soda
- ½ cup buttermilk

In large bowl of an electric mixer, beat butter and sugar until creamy; beat in egg until well combined. In another bowl, stir together flour, salt, nutmeg, and baking soda; add to butter mixture alternately with buttermilk, beating thoroughly after each addition. Gather dough into a ball, wrap tightly in plastic wrap, and refrigerate until firm (2 to 3 hours) or for up to 3 days.

On a well-floured board, roll out dough, a portion at a time, to a thickness of about ⅛ inch (keep remaining portions refrigerated). Cut out with cookie cutters (about 2½ inches in diameter) and place slightly apart on ungreased baking sheets.

Bake in a 350° oven for about 10 minutes or until lightly browned. Transfer to racks and let cool. Store airtight. Makes about 7 dozen.

Finnish Rye Cookies

(Pictured on page 46)

Rye flour gives these cookies their unusual nutty flavor. The shape is a bit unusual, too—each thin round has a small, off-center hole cut in it. In Finland, where they're a Christmas tradition, the cookies are known as *ruiskakut*.

- 1 cup rye flour
- ½ cup all-purpose flour
- ¼ teaspoon salt
- ½ cup sugar
- ½ cup (¼ lb.) firm butter or margarine, cut into pieces
- 4 tablespoons milk

In a bowl, stir together rye flour, all-purpose flour, salt, and sugar. Add butter and rub in with your fingers until mixture forms fine, even crumbs. Add milk, 1 tablespoon at a time, stirring with a fork until a stiff dough is formed. Gather dough into a ball, wrap tightly in plastic wrap, and refrigerate for 1 hour.

On a floured board, roll out dough, a portion at a time, to a thickness of about ⅛ inch. Cut out with a round cookie cutter (about 2½ inches in diameter). Then cut a hole slightly off center in each cookie, using a tiny round cutter about ½ inch in diameter (you can use the cap from a vanilla or other extract bottle). Place slightly apart on lightly greased baking sheets; prick each cookie several times with a fork.

Bake in a 375° oven for 8 to 10 minutes or until cookies are lightly browned and firm to the touch (you can bake the little cut-out holes, too—or reroll them to make more cookies). Transfer baked cookies to racks and let cool. Store airtight. Makes about 2½ dozen.

Buttery Cornmeal Wafers

Yellow cornmeal is the surprise ingredient in these tender, delicately sweet butter cookies accented with lemon. Added to the dough along with the flour, it gives the cookies a special crunch and a nutlike flavor.

    1 cup (½ lb.) butter or margarine, softened
    1 cup sugar
    2 egg yolks
    1 teaspoon grated lemon peel
 1½ cups all-purpose flour
    1 cup yellow cornmeal

In large bowl of an electric mixer, beat butter and sugar until creamy. Add egg yolks and lemon peel and beat well. In another bowl, stir together flour and cornmeal; gradually add to butter mixture, blending thoroughly. Gather dough into a ball, wrap tightly in plastic wrap, and refrigerate just until firm (about 1 hour).

Roll out dough on a well-floured board to a thickness of about ¼ inch. Cut out with cookie cutters (about 2½ inches in diameter) and place about 1 inch apart on lightly greased baking sheets. Bake in a 350° oven for 10 to 12 minutes or until edges are golden. Transfer to racks and let cool. Store airtight. Makes about 3 dozen.

Swedish Ginger Thins

(Pictured on page 46)

Very spicy, very dark, very thin, and very crisp— these are the words to describe *pepparkakor,* Sweden's version of gingersnaps. They can be cut into fancy shapes and decoratively iced for the holidays, if you like; or, if you prefer a plainer cookie, just cut them into rounds and leave them unfrosted.

 ⅔ cup butter or margarine
 ⅓ cup *each* granulated sugar and firmly
       packed brown sugar
  2 tablespoons dark corn syrup
  2 teaspoons *each* ground ginger and cloves
  3 teaspoons ground cinnamon
  2 teaspoons baking soda
 ¼ cup water
2½ cups all-purpose flour
       Royal icing (recipe follows) or
       purchased decorating icing in a
       tube or aerosol can (optional)

In a medium-size pan, combine butter, granulated sugar, brown sugar, and corn syrup; place over medium heat and stir until butter is melted. Remove from heat, stir in ginger, cloves, and cinnamon, and let cool slightly. Stir baking soda into water and add to butter mixture, blending thoroughly. Then stir in flour until well combined (dough will be quite soft). Cover tightly with plastic wrap and refrigerate until firm (2 to 3 hours) or for up to 3 days.

On a floured board, roll out dough, a portion at a time, to a thickness of about 1/16 inch. Cut out with cookie cutters (about 2½ inches in diameter). If necessary, dip cutters in flour to prevent dough from sticking to them. Place cookies slightly apart on ungreased baking sheets. Bake in a 325° oven for 10 to 12 minutes or until slightly darker brown and firm to the touch. Transfer to racks and let cool completely.

If desired, prepare royal icing. Press icing through a decorating tube with a plain tip, making swirls and outline designs on cookies. Let icing dry before storing cookies. Store airtight. Makes about 5 dozen.

Royal icing. In small bowl of an electric mixer, beat 1 **egg white** with ⅛ teaspoon **cream of tartar** and a dash of **salt** for 1 minute at high speed. Add 2 cups sifted **powdered sugar** and beat slowly until blended; then beat at high speed until very stiff (3 to 5 minutes).

Sugar Cookies

(Pictured on page 46)

Why do children love sugar cookies? Maybe it's because of their flavor, and maybe it's because they can be cut into such fancy shapes. If your youngsters like to help make sugar cookies as well as eat them, try our Easy-to-Cut Cookies—they allow the children to create their own shapes and choose decorative toppings.

- ¾ cup (¼ lb. plus 4 tablespoons) butter or margarine, softened
- 1 cup sugar
- 2 eggs
- 1 teaspoon vanilla
- 2¾ cups all-purpose flour
- 1 teaspoon *each* baking powder and salt
- Sugar

In large bowl of an electric mixer, beat butter and the 1 cup sugar until creamy; beat in eggs and vanilla. In another bowl, stir together flour, baking powder, and salt; gradually add to butter mixture, blending thoroughly, to form a soft dough. Cover tightly with plastic wrap and refrigerate until firm (at least 1 hour) or for up to 3 days.

On a floured board, roll out dough, a portion at a time, to a thickness of ⅛ inch (keep remaining portions refrigerated). Cut out with cookie cutters (about 2½ inches in diameter) and place slightly apart on ungreased baking sheets. Sprinkle generously with sugar.

Bake in a 400° oven for 8 to 10 minutes or until edges are lightly browned. Transfer to racks and let cool completely before handling. Store airtight. Makes about 4 dozen.

Easy-to-Cut Cookies

Let children choose one or more fairly simple cookie shapes—block letters, numbers, or shapes such as triangles, squares, and circles. Then trace or draw shapes on sturdy cardboard (about 1/16 inch thick), making each one about 3 by 5 inches. Cut out patterns with scissors, making sure edges are smooth.

Prepare dough as directed for **Sugar Cookies;** divide into 12 equal portions. On a floured board or directly on a lightly floured baking sheet, roll out each portion to a thickness of ⅛ inch. Let children cut around patterns with a dull knife; then lift off excess dough and set aside to reroll for additional cookies. Offer toppings such as **raisins, chocolate chips,** whole or chopped **nuts, sun-**
flower seeds, and **flaked coconut** for embellishing cookies. Bake as directed for **Sugar Cookies.** Makes about 2 dozen.

Crisp-fried Knots

(Pictured on facing page)

Cookies aren't always baked. Several cuisines feature deep-fried cookies; Italian *crespelle* and Swedish *fattigmands bakkels* are just two examples. Here's a third—*hrustule,* Yugoslavia's contribution to the collection. To Yugoslavian families, *hrustule* are special-occasion cookies, often prepared for Christmas or to celebrate festive events such as weddings. To make them, you tie strips of anise-flavored dough into loose knots, then deep-fry them to a golden crunch and dust them with powdered sugar while still warm.

- 2 eggs
- ¼ cup granulated sugar
- 2½ tablespoons brandy
- 2½ tablespoons butter or margarine, melted
- ¼ teaspoon salt
- 2 teaspoons anise seeds
- ½ teaspoon grated lemon peel
- About 2 cups all-purpose flour
- Salad oil
- Powdered sugar

In large bowl of an electric mixer, beat eggs and granulated sugar until lemon-colored. Mix in brandy, butter, salt, anise seeds, and lemon peel. Gradually stir in 1½ cups of the flour. Spread ⅓ cup more flour on a board; turn dough out onto board and knead until smooth. Wrap tightly in plastic wrap and let rest at room temperature for 30 minutes.

Work with ⅓ of the dough at a time. On a well-floured board, roll out each portion to a 6 by 30-inch rectangle (dough will be paper thin). With a pastry wheel or knife, cut into 1 by 6-inch strips; tie strips into loose knots.

Into a deep 3 to 4-quart pan, pour oil to a depth of 1 inch and heat to 360°F on a deep-frying thermometer. Add several cookies at a time and cook, turning once, until golden brown all over (about 1 minute total). Lift out cookies with a slotted spoon and let drain on paper towels. While warm, sift powdered sugar generously over tops. Serve immediately or store airtight for up to 3 days. Makes 7½ dozen.

desire). Cut a lopsided "Z" freehand down middle of each rectangle to create the two elephants (see illustration below). Then make U-shaped cuts to delineate legs; the cutouts become owls. Leave cookies on baking sheet until slightly cooled.

With a wide spatula, lift (or guide) each rectangle to a flat surface. Carefully separate elephants, taking care not to break trunks; then remove owls. Transfer carefully to racks and let cool completely. When cool, force icing through a plain tip to make toes, eyes, and ears on elephants, and eyes, beaks, and folded wings on owls. Store airtight. Makes at least 12 large elephants and 12 owls, or 96 small elephants and 96 owls.

Cut a lopsided "Z" down middle of each rectangle to create 2 elephants. Then make U-shaped cuts to delineate legs; the cutouts become owls. Icing turns the cookies into fanciful animal friends.

Sour Cream Spice Cookies

Ground coriander lends a warm, sweet spiciness to these cut-out sour cream cookies. For variety, you can top the cutouts with pine nuts and a sprinkling of sugar.

   ½ **cup (¼ lb.) butter or margarine, softened**
   1 **cup sugar**
   1 **egg**
   ½ **teaspoon** *each* **vanilla and almond extract**
   ½ **teaspoon baking soda**
   ½ **cup sour cream**
   3 **cups all-purpose flour**
1½ **teaspoons baking powder**
   ½ **teaspoon** *each* **salt and ground coriander**

In large bowl of an electric mixer, beat butter and sugar until creamy; beat in egg, vanilla, and almond extract. Stir baking soda into sour cream, then beat into butter mixture. In another bowl, stir together flour, baking powder, salt, and coriander; gradually add to butter mixture, blending thoroughly. Wrap dough tightly in plastic wrap and refrigerate until firm (about 1 hour) or for up to 3 days.

On a lightly floured board, roll out half the dough to a thickness of about ⅛ inch. Cut out with cookie cutters (about 2½ inches in diameter) and place slightly apart on ungreased baking sheets. Repeat with remaining dough. Bake in a 400° oven for 8 to 10 minutes or until golden. Transfer to racks and let cool. Store airtight. Makes about 5 dozen.

Pine Nut Sugar Cookies

Prepare dough and cut out cookies as directed for **Sour Cream Spice Cookies,** but place on greased baking sheets. Beat 1 **egg** with 1 teaspoon **water** and brush over cookies; then press **pine nuts** into surface of cookies (you'll need about ½ cup). Sprinkle cookies lightly with **sugar** and bake in a 375° oven for about 10 minutes or until edges are golden.

Brown Sugar Shortbreads

You need just four ingredients to make these buttery brown sugar cookies. As they cool, they acquire an appealing crunch.

   1 **cup (½ lb.) butter or margarine, softened**
1¼ **cups firmly packed brown sugar**
   1 **teaspoon vanilla**
2½ **cups all-purpose flour**

In large bowl of an electric mixer, beat butter and sugar until creamy. Add vanilla; then gradually beat in flour, blending thoroughly. Gather dough into a ball, wrap tightly in plastic wrap, and refrigerate until firm (about 1 hour) or for up to 3 days.

On a lightly floured board, roll out dough to a thickness of ¼ inch. Cut out with cookie cutters (about 2½ inches in diameter) and place slightly apart on lightly greased baking sheets. Bake in a 300° oven for 35 to 40 minutes or until firm to the touch (press very lightly to test). Transfer to racks and let cool. Store airtight. Makes about 3 dozen.

Spritz *(Recipe on facing page)*

1 Assemble press according to manufacturer's directions, selecting design plate(s) you wish to use. Fill press with dough, packing it in firmly.

2 For snowflakes, stand press on baking sheet; turn handle to shape dough. To release cookie, turn handle slightly in reverse direction and lift press.

3 For rosettes, use star plate. Hold press at an angle and release dough in a spiral, working from the center out.

4 For ribbons, use ridged plate to form long strips of dough. Cut into 2½-inch lengths; separate lengths slightly. Press down gently to release any air bubbles.

Pressed Cookies

Pressed cookies are made from soft doughs or batters that are forced through a cookie press or pastry bag to make fancy shapes. Perhaps more than any other technique in cookiedom, this one yields professional-looking results—though you may need to practice a little before you can turn out perfect cookies with ease. Cookie presses and pastry bags are available in cookware shops and some hardware stores, and often through mail-order catalogues.

Spritz
(Pictured on facing page)

Buttery, almond-flavored Swedish spritz are probably the best known pressed cookies. Though they're often baked for the holidays, they're just as good at any other time of year. You can make spritz in a variety of fancy shapes, depending on which design plate you choose, and dress them up with candied fruit, colored sugar, silver dragées, or other decorations.

> 1 cup (½ lb.) butter, softened
> ¾ cup sugar
> 2 egg yolks
> 1 teaspoon vanilla
> ½ teaspoon almond extract
> 2½ cups all-purpose flour
> ½ teaspoon baking powder
> ⅛ teaspoon salt
> Decorations (suggestions follow)

In large bowl of an electric mixer, beat butter until creamy. Gradually add sugar, beating until fluffy. Add egg yolks, one at a time, and beat until smooth. Beat in vanilla and almond extract. In another bowl, stir together flour, baking powder, and salt; gradually add to butter mixture, blending thoroughly.

Place dough in a cookie press fitted with a design plate, packing it in firmly and evenly. Force out onto ungreased baking sheets, spacing cookies about 1 inch apart. If kitchen is very warm and dough is soft and sticky, refrigerate until firm enough to press easily. Decorate as desired.

Bake in a 350° oven for 12 to 15 minutes or until edges are lightly browned. Transfer to racks and let cool. Store airtight. Makes about 4 dozen.

Decorations. Before baking, top cookies with halved **candied cherries;** or sprinkle with finely chopped **nuts, colored sugar, nonpareils, silver dragées,** or **chocolate sprinkles.** Or brush baked cookies with this chocolate glaze: in top of a double boiler over simmering water, melt together 4 ounces **semisweet chocolate** and ½ teaspoon **solid vegetable shortening.** Apply with a pastry brush. Refrigerate glazed cookies for 10 minutes to harden glaze.

Swiss Almond Macaroons

Snowy with powdered sugar, these Swiss-style macaroons have a crisp surface and a chewy, lemon-flavored center. To get the crackled surface that marks the Swiss touch, let the unbaked cookies dry at room temperature for 8 to 24 hours; then pinch tops and bake.

> 8 ounces almond paste
> 1 cup plus 2 tablespoons granulated sugar
> 1 teaspoon grated lemon peel
> About ⅓ cup egg whites (whites of about 3 large eggs)
> About ½ cup powdered sugar

In large bowl of an electric mixer, beat almond paste, granulated sugar, and lemon peel until mixture resembles very fine crumbs. Gradually drizzle in egg whites, blending well after each addition, until batter just barely holds soft peaks.

Stand a pastry bag fitted with a plain tip (#6 size) in a drinking glass; then fill it with batter. Pipe onto baking sheets lined with parchment paper or brown wrapping paper, making 1¼-inch circles spaced 2 inches apart. (If batter is so thin that it runs out of bag, spoon it onto baking sheets by rounded teaspoonfuls.)

Sift powdered sugar generously over each round to cover completely. Let unbaked cookies stand, uncovered, until they're dry enough to develop a slight crust (at least 8 hours or up to 24 hours).

Pinch top of each round simultaneously with thumb and forefinger of both hands, making 4 indentations. Bake on center rack in a 350° oven for 12 to 15 minutes or until richly golden. Slide parchment and macaroons off baking sheet onto a damp towel and let cool. Run a spatula under cookies to loosen from parchment. Store airtight. Makes about 3½ dozen.

Ladyfingers

Feathery-light and luscious, ladyfingers are among the world's daintiest cookies. They make a lovely accompaniment for a cup of tea, and can also be used in the preparation of classic desserts such as charlottes.

      Cornstarch
  ¾ cup plus 1 tablespoon all-purpose flour
      Dash of salt
  ⅔ cup sugar
  4 eggs
  1 teaspoon vanilla

Grease 2 baking sheets, then dust with cornstarch and set aside.

Sift flour, measure, and sift again with salt and ⅓ cup of the sugar; set aside.

Separate eggs. In large bowl of an electric mixer, beat whites until stiff, beating in remaining ⅓ cup sugar, 1 tablespoon at a time. In small bowl of mixer, beat yolks with vanilla until thick and lemon-colored. Fold yolk mixture into beaten whites. Sift flour mixture over eggs; carefully fold in.

Stand a pastry bag fitted with a plain tip (#7 size) in a drinking glass; fill with batter. Pipe batter onto prepared baking sheets, forming fingers about 1 by 4 inches; space fingers about 1 inch apart. (Or spoon batter into greased and cornstarch-dusted ladyfinger pans.)

Bake in a 350° oven for 9 to 10 minutes or until lightly browned. Let cool on baking sheets (or in pans) for about a minute, then transfer to racks and let cool completely. Store airtight. Makes 2½ dozen.

Filled Cookies

To make these elaborate treats, you begin by rolling out dough with a rolling pin as you would for cut-out cookies (page 48). Then, however, you wrap it around a filling, using cutting and shaping techniques that vary from recipe to recipe. What you end up with might be anything from a horn to a turnover—or even a special little cookie that looks like ravioli.

If you like making filled cookies, you might also want to try Fruit Newtons (page 79), Date Tarts (page 80), and Raspberry-Nut Valentines (page 84).

Flaky Fruit Turnovers

(Pictured on page 46)

A rich butter pastry distinguishes these tender, triangular turnover cookies; tucked inside is a dried-fruit filling made of apricots or dates. The cookies freeze well, so consider baking a batch of each kind and putting some away.

  2 cups all-purpose flour
  ¼ cup sugar
  1 cup (½ lb.) firm butter or margarine, cut into pieces
  ⅓ cup milk
      Apricot or date filling (recipes follow)

In a bowl, combine flour and sugar. Add butter; with your fingers or a pastry blender, rub or cut mixture until it forms fine, even crumbs. Gradually add milk, mixing with a fork until dough holds together. Cover tightly with plastic wrap and refrigerate for 30 minutes to 1 hour. Meanwhile, prepare filling of your choice.

Divide dough in half; form each half into a ball. On a well-floured board, roll out one ball into a 12-inch square, then cut it into sixteen 3-inch squares (press straight down with a long-bladed knife to make neat cookies). Mound a scant teaspoon of filling in the center of each square. Fold each over into a triangle and seal by running a pastry wheel around edges or crimping them with the tines of a fork. Repeat with remaining dough.

Transfer cookies to ungreased baking sheets. If desired, use a small, sharp knife to cut a small slash in each cookie to expose filling. Bake in a 350° oven for 18 to 20 minutes or until golden brown. Transfer to racks and let cool. Store airtight. Makes 32.

Apricot filling. In a small pan, combine ½ cup firmly packed chopped **dried apricots,** ⅔ cup **water,** and ¼ cup firmly packed **brown sugar.** Cook over medium heat, stirring constantly and mashing with a spoon, until mixture forms a smooth, thick paste (about 10 minutes). Let cool to room temperature.

Date filling. In a small pan, combine ½ cup firmly packed snipped **pitted dates,** ½ teaspoon grated **lemon peel,** 3 tablespoons **lemon juice,** ½ cup **water,** and ¼ cup firmly packed **brown sugar.** Cook over medium heat, stirring constantly and mashing with a spoon, until mixture forms a smooth, thick paste (about 10 minutes). Let cool to room temperature.

Russian Walnut Horns

A cinnamon-spiced ground walnut filling rests snugly inside these "horns" of sweet yeast pastry. Powdered sugar lends a bakeshop-fancy finish.

2¾ cups all-purpose flour
¼ teaspoon salt
1 cup (½ lb.) firm butter or margarine, cut into pieces
1 package active dry yeast
¼ cup warm water (about 110°F)
2 eggs
½ cup sour cream
Walnut filling (recipe follows)
About ⅓ cup *each* all-purpose flour and granulated sugar
Powdered sugar

In a large mixing bowl, stir together the 2¾ cups flour and salt. With a pastry blender or 2 knives, cut in butter until mixture resembles cornmeal; set aside.

Dissolve yeast in warm water. Separate eggs; set whites aside and beat yolks until light and lemon-colored. Add dissolved yeast and ¼ cup of the sour cream to yolks, stirring until blended; stir yolk mixture into flour mixture.

In another bowl, using clean, dry beaters, beat egg whites until stiff but not dry. Fold remaining ¼ cup sour cream into whites, then add to flour mixture, blending thoroughly (dough will be sticky). Cover tightly with plastic wrap and refrigerate until firm (2 to 3 hours). Meanwhile, prepare walnut filling; cover and set aside.

Stir together the ⅓ cup flour and granulated sugar; sprinkle enough of the mixture over a board to coat generously. Divide dough into portions about the size of baseballs. Roll out one portion to a rectangle about ⅛ inch thick (keep remaining portions refrigerated). With a pastry wheel or sharp knife, cut into 2-inch squares. For tender cookies, handle the dough as little as possible.

Place a scant teaspoon of filling in the center of each square. Fold 2 opposite corners of square into center, overlapping dough and pinching firmly to seal. Place horns slightly apart on ungreased baking sheets. Repeat with remaining dough, sprinkling board with more flour-sugar mixture as necessary.

Bake in a 350° oven for 15 minutes or until lightly browned. Transfer to racks and let cool slightly; while still warm, sift powdered sugar over cookies to cover lightly. Store airtight. Makes about 8 dozen.

Walnut filling. Stir together 1⅓ cups ground **walnuts** (whirled fine in a food processor or blender), ⅔ cup **sugar,** ¾ teaspoon **ground cinnamon,** and 4 teaspoons **melted butter.** Add **milk,** a few drops at a time, just until mixture binds together loosely (you'll need 1 to 2 teaspoons).

Almond Ravioli Cookies

(Pictured on page 46)

We borrowed a technique from Italian cooking to make these little almond-filled bites.

1 cup (½ lb.) butter or margarine, softened
1½ cups powdered sugar
1 egg
1 teaspoon vanilla
2½ cups all-purpose flour
1 teaspoon *each* baking soda and cream of tartar
About ⅔ cup (6 oz.) almond paste
About ⅓ cup sliced almonds

In large bowl of an electric mixer, beat butter and sugar until creamy; beat in egg and vanilla. In another bowl, stir together flour, baking soda, and cream of tartar; gradually add to butter mixture, blending thoroughly. Divide dough in half. Wrap each half tightly in plastic wrap and refrigerate until firm (2 to 3 hours) or for up to 3 days.

Place one portion of dough between 2 pieces of wax paper and roll out into a 10 by 15-inch rectangle. Peel off and discard top paper.

With a pastry wheel or a long-bladed knife, lightly mark dough into 1-inch squares. Place a small ball of almond paste (use a scant ¼ teaspoon for each) in the center of each square; refrigerate while rolling top layer.

Repeat rolling procedure for second portion of dough. Peel off and discard top paper. Invert sheet of dough onto almond-paste-topped dough. Peel off and discard paper. Gently press top layer of dough around mounds of filling.

Flour a pastry wheel or sharp knife and cut filled dough into 1-inch squares, then run pastry wheel around outer edges to seal (or press with fingers). Place cookies about 1 inch apart on ungreased baking sheets. Push a sliced almond diagonally into the center of each cookie.

Bake in a 350° oven for 10 to 12 minutes or until golden. Transfer to racks and let cool. Store airtight. Makes about 12½ dozen.

Viennese Jam Rounds

(Pictured on page 46)

These fancy cookies resemble stained-glass windows; before baking, each one is crowned with a bit of jam and two crisscrossed dough strips.

> 1 cup (½ lb.) butter or margarine, softened
> 1 cup sugar
> 2 egg yolks
> 1 teaspoon grated lemon peel
> 2 cups all-purpose flour
> ¼ teaspoon salt
> ¾ teaspoon ground cinnamon
> ¼ teaspoon ground cloves
> 1 cup ground almonds
> About ½ cup raspberry or apricot jam

In large bowl of an electric mixer, beat butter and sugar until creamy. Beat in egg yolks and lemon peel. In another bowl, stir together flour, salt, cinnamon, and cloves; gradually add to butter mixture, blending thoroughly. Stir in almonds (dough will be very stiff). Gather dough into a ball, wrap tightly in plastic wrap, and refrigerate for 1 hour.

Divide dough in half. Roll each half between 2 pieces of wax paper to a thickness of ⅛ inch. Cut out with a 2-inch round cookie cutter and place about 2 inches apart on ungreased baking sheets. Top each cookie with about ½ teaspoon jam, spreading to within about ½ inch of edges. Cut dough scraps (reroll, if necessary) into ¼ by 2-inch strips; cross 2 strips over top of each cookie and press ends down lightly.

Bake in a 375° oven for about 12 minutes or until edges are browned. Let cool for about a minute on baking sheets, then transfer to racks and let cool completely. Store airtight. Makes about 4 dozen.

Cookie-iron Cookies

Cookies shaped with cookie irons are specialty items indeed. Scandinavian rosettes and *krumkake*, French *gaufrettes*, Italian *pizelle*, and the Dutch *siroop wafel* all belong to this category.

Rosettes must be made with a rosette iron, a long-handled metal mold with a decorative shape. The other cookies are all made in hinged waffle-type irons—so, though each type has its own special iron, you can use recipes and irons inter-changeably. Just be sure to adjust the amount of batter to suit the size iron you're using.

New waffle-type irons that don't have a nonstick fluorocarbon finish must be seasoned before you make cookies. To season an iron, place it directly over medium heat (on a gas or electric range) until water dripped inside sizzles. Open and brush generously with salad oil, then close and heat just until oil smokes. Remove from heat; let cool in the open position. Wipe clean.

Even if your iron does have a nonstick finish, brush it with melted butter before baking the first few cookies in each batch.

Krumkake

(Pictured on facing page)

Scandinavian *krumkake* irons produce cookies embossed with delicate scrollwork.

> 3 eggs
> ½ cup sugar
> 6 tablespoons butter or margarine, melted
> ½ teaspoon lemon extract
> ½ teaspoon ground cardamom (optional)
> ⅔ cup all-purpose flour
> Melted butter or margarine
> Whipped cream (optional)

In a bowl, beat eggs with sugar, the 6 tablespoons butter, lemon extract, and cardamom (if used). Add flour and stir until mixture is smooth.

Place a seasoned krumkake iron (5 or 6 inches in diameter) directly over medium-high heat. Alternately heat both sides of iron until water dripped inside sizzles. Open and brush lightly with melted butter. Reduce heat to medium.

Spoon batter down center of iron (you'll need 1 to 3 tablespoons, depending on size of iron). Close and squeeze handles together; scrape off and discard any batter that flows out. Bake, turning about every 20 seconds and opening often to check doneness, until cookie is light golden brown. Remove iron from heat and lift out cookie with a fork, spatula, or tongs.

Working quickly, shape hot cookie into a cone or roll into a cylinder (or leave flat, if you prefer). Place on a rack to cool. Return iron to heat and repeat with remaining batter. Store cookies airtight; serve plain or fill with whipped cream just before serving. Makes about 1½ dozen 5-inch cookies.

Krumkake *(Recipe on facing page)*

1 Spoon batter down center of iron; you'll need 1 to 3 table-spoons per cookie, de-pending on size of iron.

2 Close iron and squeeze handles together. Remove from heat and scrape off any batter that flows out.

3 Return to heat and bake, turning iron about every 20 seconds. When cookie is golden, lift out of iron with a fork, spatula, or tongs.

4 Working quickly, shape hot cookie into a cone—or leave flat, if you prefer. Let cool on a rack.

Pizelle

Italian *pizelle* start with a dough that you shape by hand before baking it in an iron. The baked cookies have a star design and a lemon-anise flavor.

   3 **eggs**
   ¾ **cup sugar**
   ¾ **cup (¼ lb. plus 4 tablespoons) butter or margarine, melted**
   1 **teaspoon lemon extract**
   ¾ **teaspoon** *each* **baking powder and anise seeds**
   3½ **cups all-purpose flour**
      Melted butter or margarine

Beat eggs until thick. Add sugar, the ¾ cup butter, lemon extract, baking powder, anise seeds, and flour; mix well.

Place a seasoned pizelle iron (about 5 inches in diameter) directly over medium-high heat. Alternately heat both sides of iron until water dripped inside sizzles. Open and brush lightly with melted butter.

Shape dough into balls, using 2 to 4 tablespoons for each, depending on size of iron. Place a ball of dough in center of iron (roll into a rope if using a rectangular iron). Close and squeeze handles together; turn iron. Bake, turning about every 20 seconds and opening often to check doneness, until cookie is light golden brown. Quickly lift out cookie with a fork or spatula; place flat on a rack to cool. Return iron to heat and repeat with remaining dough. Store cookies airtight. Makes about 1½ dozen.

Gaufrettes

A tiny wafflelike pattern is characteristic of French *gaufrettes*. After baking, each cookie is cut in half to make two little squares, which happen to make excellent ice cream sandwiches—just place a slice of your favorite ice cream in between.

   ½ **pint (1 cup) whipping cream**
   1 **cup all-purpose flour**
   ¾ **cup powdered sugar**
   2 **teaspoons vanilla**
   ¼ **teaspoon salt**
      Melted butter or margarine

In small bowl of an electric mixer, beat cream just until it begins to thicken; then add flour, sugar, vanilla, and salt and blend until mixture is smooth.

Place a seasoned gaufrette iron directly over medium-high heat. Alternately heat both sides of iron until water dripped inside sizzles. Open and brush lightly with melted butter.

Spoon batter down center of iron (you'll need 1 to 3 tablespoons, depending on size of iron). Close and squeeze handles together; scrape off and discard any batter that flows out. Bake, turning about every 20 seconds and opening often to check doneness, until cookie is light golden brown. Remove iron from heat and lift out cookie with a fork, spatula, or tongs. While cookie is still hot, cut in half crosswise and place on a rack to cool. Repeat with remaining batter. Store cookies airtight. Makes about 2 dozen.

Rosettes

With a rosette iron, you can produce unusual deep-fried batter cookies with an airy snowflake design. You preheat the iron in hot oil, dip it in batter, and then plunge it back into the oil until the cookie turns golden—it takes only a few seconds. The irons are available in cookware shops; most come with interchangeable molds, so you can vary the shape of the cookies.

   ½ **cup cornstarch**
   2 **tablespoons all-purpose flour**
   2 **teaspoons granulated sugar**
   1 **teaspoon ground cinnamon or 1½ teaspoons ground cardamom**
   ½ **teaspoon salt**
   1 **egg**
   ¼ **cup milk**
      Salad oil
      Powdered sugar

In a bowl, stir together cornstarch, flour, granulated sugar, cinnamon, and salt. Beat egg lightly, combine with milk, and add to dry ingredients. Stir until batter is smooth.

Into a deep, heavy pan about 6 inches in diameter, pour oil to a depth of about 1½ inches and heat to 375°F on a deep-frying thermometer. For each rosette, preheat iron in oil; then dip hot iron into batter nearly up to (but not over) top. If batter does not adhere to iron, temperature of iron or oil is too hot or too cold.

Lower iron into oil for about 10 seconds or until rosette is lightly browned. Remove from oil, gently loosen rosette from iron with a fork, and drain on paper towels. Repeat with remaining batter. When rosettes are completely cooled, sift powdered sugar over them. Store airtight. Makes about 1½ dozen.

Gouda Syrup Waffles

The same Dutch community that gives Gouda cheese its name also has a cookie to its credit: the syrup waffle (*stroop* or *siroop wafel* in Dutch). It's made of vanilla wafers baked in a cookie iron, then sandwiched around a thick, golden caramel filling for a cookie that's crisp on the outside, chewy on the inside.

In Gouda and some other Dutch cities, mainly on national holidays and at fairs, street vendors bake the cookies while you watch; warm and freshly made, they're a true delight. More typically, however, you buy the syrup waffles packaged in cellophane or cans at pastry shops or grocery stores. In Dutch homes, syrup waffles are served for birthdays and feast days, or as a special treat with morning coffee.

You can make syrup waffles at home, using any waffle-type cookie iron to bake the wafers. A gaufrette iron gives the most authentic appearance, but pizelle and krumkake irons work well, too.

    2   cups all-purpose flour
    ½   cup sugar
    1½ teaspoons baking powder
    ¼   teaspoon salt
    4   tablespoons butter or margarine, melted
    2   eggs, lightly beaten
    1   teaspoon vanilla
        Melted butter or margarine
        Caramel syrup (recipe follows)

In a large mixing bowl, stir together flour, sugar, baking powder, and salt. Add the 4 tablespoons butter, eggs, and vanilla; with a wooden spoon or your hands, work dough until well blended. Form into a ball, wrap tightly in plastic wrap, and refrigerate until firm (at least 1 hour).

Divide dough into 50 equal portions; roll each into a ball. Place a seasoned gaufrette iron or other waffle-type cookie iron directly over medium-high heat. Alternately heat both sides of iron until water dripped inside sizzles. Open and brush lightly with melted butter. Place a ball of dough in iron; close. Bake, turning about every 20 seconds and opening often to check doneness, until cookie is golden brown (about 1 minute). Quickly lift out cookie with a fork or spatula and transfer to a rack to cool. Repeat with remaining dough.

Prepare caramel syrup. To assemble syrup waffles, spread warm syrup on one wafer, then top with another; gently press together. Store airtight. Makes 25 filled wafers.

Caramel syrup. In a 2-quart pan, combine ½ pint (1 cup) **whipping cream,** 1 cup firmly packed **brown sugar,** and ¼ cup **light corn syrup.** Boil over medium-high heat, uncovered, stirring occasionally, until a candy thermometer registers 238°F. Let cool briefly (just until thick enough to spread). If caramel becomes too thick, set pan in hot water and stir until spreadable.

Cookies for Young Bakers

Children love to eat cookies any time, but especially when they've helped in the baking. The cookies listed below are good choices for those times when you have a small pair of helping hands in the kitchen; they involve techniques that children enjoy and can manage easily.

Icebox Cookies

For the baker whose time is limited, icebox cookies are a boon indeed, offering make-ahead ease and adaptability. Sometimes called refrigerator cookies or slice-and-bake cookies, they're made by forming the dough into long rolls or logs, refrigerating it until firm, and then slicing it crosswise into cookies ready for baking. This method is appealing to many because the dough can be prepared days or even weeks in advance (it freezes well); slicing and baking take little time and can be done at your convenience.

The icebox technique generally yields uniform, waferlike cookies with a crisp texture. If you want cookies with decorated edges, just roll the log of dough in sugar or nuts before chilling. Or adapt the technique to produce more elaborate results; by rolling the dough around a filling or stacking different kinds of dough, you can turn out fancy treats such as pinwheels (pages 66, 68, and 69) and two-toned striped cookies (page 66).

Photo at left *offers a look at our galaxy of icebox cookies. From inside out: Danish Sugar Cookies (page 64), Spiced Almond Thins (page 65), Lemon-Pecan Wafers (page 65), Peanut Pinwheels (page 69), Coconut Shortbread Cookies (page 68), Poppy Seed Nut Slices (page 65), Date-Oatmeal Cookies (page 69), and Danish Sugar Cookies.*

Danish Sugar Cookies

(Pictured on page 62)

Denmark is well known for the quality of her pastry and cookies, and these little treats will show you why. Crisp, sugary edges and a ground-almond dough make them special.

> 1 **cup sugar**
> ½ **cup (¼ lb.) firm butter, cut into pieces**
> ½ **cup whole blanched almonds, finely ground**
> 1 **teaspoon vanilla**
> 1 **cup all-purpose flour**
> **Sugar**

Place the 1 cup sugar in a large bowl; cut in butter with a pastry blender or 2 knives until mixture forms fine particles. Stir in almonds and vanilla. Blend in flour, mixing with your hands if necessary, until well combined. Shape dough into a roll 1½ inches in diameter. Sprinkle a little sugar (1 to 2 tablespoons) on a sheet of wax paper; then place roll of dough on paper and wrap snugly, coating outside of roll with sugar. Refrigerate until firm (at least 2 hours) or for up to 3 days.

Unwrap dough. Using a sharp knife, cut into ⅛-inch-thick slices. Place slices slightly apart on ungreased baking sheets. Bake in a 375° oven for 8 to 10 minutes or until lightly browned. Let cool on baking sheets for about a minute, then transfer to racks and let cool completely. Store airtight. Makes about 5 dozen.

French Butter Wafers

Crisp and fragile butter wafers, accented only with vanilla, are elegant in their simplicity. Since the butter provides much of their delicate flavor, it's best not to substitute margarine in this recipe.

> 1 **cup (½ lb.) butter, softened**
> 1¼ **cups powdered sugar**
> 1 **egg**
> 1 **teaspoon vanilla**
> 2 **cups all-purpose flour**
> 1 **teaspoon *each* baking soda and cream of tartar**
> ⅛ **teaspoon salt**

In large bowl of an electric mixer, beat butter until creamy. Beat in sugar; add egg and vanilla and beat well. In another bowl, stir together flour, baking soda, cream of tartar, and salt; gradually add to butter mixture, blending thoroughly. Shape dough into a roll 1½ inches in diameter; wrap in wax paper and refrigerate until firm (at least 2 hours) or for up to 3 days.

Unwrap dough. Using a sharp knife, cut into ⅜-inch-thick slices; place slices 2 inches apart on ungreased baking sheets. Bake in a 350° oven for 10 to 12 minutes or until golden. Let cool on baking sheets for about a minute, then transfer to racks and let cool completely. Store airtight. Makes about 4 dozen.

Candied Ginger Crisps

Tiny nuggets of candied ginger are a piquant surprise in these dark, spicy coconut cookies. They're especially delicious alongside fruit salad or ice cream. Candied ginger (sometimes called crystallized ginger) is available in most well-stocked supermarkets.

> ½ **cup (¼ lb.) butter or margarine, softened**
> ½ **cup solid vegetable shortening**
> 1 **cup sugar**
> ½ **cup light molasses**
> 3 **cups all-purpose flour**
> 1 **teaspoon *each* baking soda, ground ginger, and ground cinnamon**
> ½ **teaspoon ground cloves**
> 1 **cup flaked coconut**
> ½ **cup finely chopped candied ginger**

In large bowl of an electric mixer, beat butter, shortening, and sugar until creamy; beat in molasses. In another bowl, stir together flour, baking soda, ground ginger, cinnamon, and cloves; gradually add to butter mixture, blending thoroughly. Add coconut and candied ginger and mix until well combined. Shape dough into 2 or 3 rolls, each 1½ inches in diameter; wrap in wax paper and refrigerate until firm (at least 4 hours) or for up to 3 days.

Unwrap dough. Using a sharp knife, cut into ¼-inch-thick slices; place slices about 1 inch apart on lightly greased baking sheets. Bake in a 350° oven for 10 minutes or until edges are lightly browned. Transfer to racks and let cool. Store airtight. Makes about 7 dozen.

Lemon-Pecan Wafers

(Pictured on page 62)

Here's a good summertime cookie. Though rich with butter and nuts, it has a refreshing, lemony sparkle.

- ½ cup (¼ lb.) butter or margarine, softened
- 1 cup sugar
- 1 egg
- 1 tablespoon *each* grated lemon peel and lemon juice
- 2 cups all-purpose flour
- ⅛ teaspoon salt
- 1 teaspoon baking powder
- 1 cup chopped pecans

In large bowl of an electric mixer, beat butter and sugar until creamy; beat in egg, lemon peel, and lemon juice. In another bowl, stir together flour, salt, and baking powder; gradually add to butter mixture, blending thoroughly. Stir in pecans, mixing with your hands if necessary to distribute nuts evenly. Shape dough into 2 rolls, each 1½ inches in diameter; wrap in wax paper and refrigerate until firm (at least 2 hours) or for up to 3 days.

Unwrap dough. Using a sharp knife, cut into ⅛-inch-thick slices; place slices about 1 inch apart on greased baking sheets. Bake in a 350° oven for 12 minutes or until edges are lightly browned. Transfer to racks and let cool. Store airtight. Makes about 6 dozen.

Spiced Almond Thins

(Pictured on page 62)

Sour cream, brown sugar, cinnamon, and nutmeg combine in a crisp spice wafer with an appealing old-fashioned flavor. Crunchy bits of almond give the cookies a pebbly appearance.

- 1 cup (½ lb.) butter or margarine, softened
- 1 cup firmly packed brown sugar
- 2 cups all-purpose flour
- 2 teaspoons ground cinnamon
- ½ teaspoon ground nutmeg
- ¼ teaspoon baking soda
- ¼ cup sour cream
- ½ cup slivered blanched almonds

In large bowl of an electric mixer, beat butter and sugar until creamy. In another bowl, stir together flour, cinnamon, and nutmeg. Stir baking soda into sour cream; add to butter mixture alternately with flour mixture, blending thoroughly. Stir in almonds until well combined. Shape dough into a 2½-inch-thick rectangular log; wrap in wax paper and refrigerate until firm (at least 2 hours) or for up to 3 days.

Unwrap dough. Using a sharp knife, cut into ⅛-inch-thick slices; place slices about 1 inch apart on ungreased baking sheets. Bake in a 350° oven for 10 minutes or until golden brown. Let cool for about a minute on baking sheets, then transfer to racks and let cool completely. Store airtight. Makes about 5 dozen.

Poppy Seed Nut Slices

(Pictured on page 62)

Hazelnuts and poppy seeds team up to give these crunchy little cookies their distinctive flavor. If you like hazelnuts, you might also enjoy the chocolate-dipped bonbons on page 40 and the nut shortbread on page 74.

- 1 cup (½ lb.) butter or margarine, softened
- 1 cup sugar
- 1 egg
- 1 teaspoon vanilla
- 2½ cups all-purpose flour
- ⅓ cup poppy seeds
- ½ teaspoon ground cinnamon
- ¼ teaspoon *each* salt and ground ginger
- 1½ cups coarsely chopped hazelnuts (filberts)

In large bowl of an electric mixer, beat butter and sugar until creamy; beat in egg and vanilla. In another bowl, stir together flour, poppy seeds, cinnamon, salt, and ginger; gradually add to butter mixture, blending thoroughly. Add hazelnuts, mixing with your hands if necessary to distribute nuts evenly. Shape dough into 2 or 3 rolls, each 1½ inches in diameter; wrap in wax paper and refrigerate until firm (at least 2 hours) or for up to 3 days.

Unwrap dough. Using a sharp knife, cut into ¼-inch-thick slices; place slices about 1 inch apart on ungreased baking sheets. Bake in a 350° oven for 12 to 15 minutes or until edges are golden. Transfer to racks and let cool. Store airtight. Makes about 7 dozen.

Cinnamon Pinwheels

In their buttery flavor and crisp, flaky texture, these cookies resemble puff pastry. They're made from slices of yeast dough swirled with sweet cinnamon filling; each slice is rolled out into a large, thin circle and sprinkled generously with sugar before baking.

      3 cups all-purpose flour
      ½ teaspoon salt
      1 teaspoon ground cardamom (optional)
      2 tablespoons sugar
      1 cup (½ lb.) firm butter or margarine,
         cut into pieces
      1 package active dry yeast
      ¼ cup warm water (about 110°F)
      ½ cup milk
      1 egg, lightly beaten
      3 tablespoons salad oil
         Cinnamon filling (recipe follows)
         Sugar

In a large mixing bowl, combine flour, salt, cardamom (if used), and the 2 tablespoons sugar. With a pastry blender or 2 knives, cut butter into flour mixture until particles are about the size of peas.

Dissolve yeast in water; then stir in milk, egg, and oil. With a fork, stir yeast mixture into flour mixture just until flour is moistened. Cover tightly with plastic wrap and refrigerate until cold (about 2 hours). Meanwhile, prepare cinnamon filling and set aside.

Turn dough out onto a lightly floured board; knead gently, 4 times only. Roll out to an 11 by 18-inch rectangle, keeping sides straight. Sprinkle filling evenly over surface to within ¼ inch of each edge. Starting with a long edge, roll up jelly roll style; pinch seam to seal. Wrap in wax paper and refrigerate until firm (at least 2 hours) or for up to 3 days.

Cut filled and rolled dough crosswise into fourths; return 3 rolls to refrigerator. Using a sharp knife, cut remaining portion into ½-inch-thick slices. On a well-floured board, roll each slice out with a floured rolling pin into a circle about 5 inches in diameter, adding more flour as needed to prevent sticking. (If kitchen is warm, keep unrolled slices in refrigerator until needed.)

Place circles close together on ungreased baking sheets and sprinkle generously with sugar. Bake in a 350° oven for 15 minutes or until golden brown. Transfer to racks and let cool. Repeat with remaining dough. Store airtight. Makes 3 dozen.

Cinnamon filling. In a bowl, stir together ¼ cup firmly packed **brown sugar** and 2 tablespoons *each* **granulated sugar** and **ground cinnamon.**

Black & White Slices
(Pictured on facing page)

Jaunty stripes of vanilla and chocolate-flavored dough give these little squares a festive appearance. If you like, you can experiment with combining the doughs in other shapes—try making checkerboards, pinwheels, or half moons.

      ½ cup (¼ lb.) butter or margarine, softened
      ½ cup sugar
      1 egg yolk
     1½ cups all-purpose flour
     1½ teaspoons baking powder
      ⅛ teaspoon salt
      3 tablespoons milk
      ½ teaspoon vanilla
      1 square (1 oz.) unsweetened chocolate

In large bowl of an electric mixer, beat butter and sugar until creamy; beat in egg yolk. In another bowl, stir together flour, baking powder, and salt. In a small cup, combine milk and vanilla. Add dry ingredients to butter mixture alternately with milk mixture, blending thoroughly after each addition.

In top of a double boiler over simmering water or in a small pan over lowest possible heat, melt chocolate, stirring constantly; let cool slightly. Divide dough in half; take 1 tablespoon dough from one half and add it to the other half. Stir chocolate into smaller portion of dough, blending until well combined.

Shape each portion of dough into a roll 1½ inches in diameter. Wrap each in wax paper; flatten sides to make square logs. Refrigerate until firm (at least 2 hours) or for up to 3 days.

Unwrap dough. Using a sharp knife, slice each log lengthwise into fourths. Then reassemble logs, using 2 dark slices and 2 light slices for each, alternating colors to make stripes. Gently press layers together to eliminate interior air pockets.

Cut logs crosswise into ⅛-inch-thick slices (if layers start to separate, refrigerate until dough is firmer). Place slices about 1 inch apart on greased baking sheets. Bake in a 350° oven for about 10 minutes or until light golden. Transfer to racks and let cool. Store airtight. Makes about 4 dozen.

Black & White Slices *(Recipe on facing page)*

1 Form each portion of dough into a roll and wrap in wax paper; flatten sides to make square logs. Chill until firm.

2 Unwrap chilled logs and slice lengthwise into quarters, using a sharp knife.

3 Reassemble logs, alternating dark and light portions to make stripes. Press layers together gently as you work.

4 With a sharp knife, cut logs crosswise into ⅛-inch-thick slices; place on greased baking sheets.

Coconut Shortbread Cookies

(Pictured on page 62)

Is it possible to improve on traditional Scottish shortbread? One taste of these meltingly rich cookies may convince you to answer "yes." Lots of coconut is added to a basic shortbread dough for an irresistible cross-cultural treat.

- 1 cup (½ lb.) butter, softened
- ¼ cup granulated sugar
- 1 teaspoon vanilla
- 2 cups all-purpose flour
- ¼ teaspoon salt
- 2 cups flaked coconut
- About 1 cup powdered sugar

In large bowl of an electric mixer, beat butter until creamy; add granulated sugar and beat until smooth. Mix in vanilla. In another bowl, stir together flour and salt; gradually add to butter mixture, blending thoroughly. Add coconut and mix until well combined. Shape dough into a roll about 1½ inches in diameter; wrap in wax paper and refrigerate until firm (at least 2 hours) or for up to 3 days.

Unwrap dough. Using a sharp knife, cut into ¼-inch-thick slices; place slices slightly apart on ungreased baking sheets. Bake in a 300° oven for 20 minutes or until cookies are firm to the touch and lightly browned on bottoms. Transfer to racks and let cool for 5 minutes. Sift half the powdered sugar onto wax paper and transfer cookies to it in a single layer; sift additional powdered sugar on top to cover cookies lightly. Let cookies cool completely. Store airtight. Makes about 4 dozen.

Peanut Butter & Jam Cookies

Kids will love these jam-filled cookies as a warm-from-the-oven snack or a lunchbox dessert. You make them by sandwiching a spoonful of your favorite preserves between two slices of refrigerator dough, then crimping the edges to seal the filling inside.

For variety, try substituting five or six semi-sweet chocolate, butterscotch, or peanut butter-flavored chips for the jam in each cookie.

- 1½ cups all-purpose flour
- ½ cup sugar
- ½ teaspoon baking soda
- ¼ teaspoon salt
- ½ cup *each* solid vegetable shortening and peanut butter
- ¼ cup light corn syrup
- 1 tablespoon milk
- About ½ cup jam (strawberry, raspberry, apricot, or other fruit flavor)

In a large mixing bowl, combine flour, sugar, baking soda, and salt. With a pastry blender or 2 knives, cut in shortening and peanut butter until mixture forms moist, even crumbs. Stir in corn syrup and milk until blended. Shape dough into a roll 2 inches in diameter; wrap in wax paper and refrigerate until firm (at least 3 hours) or for up to 3 days.

Unwrap dough. Using a sharp knife, cut into ⅛-inch-thick slices. Place half the slices slightly apart on ungreased baking sheets and top each with ½ teaspoon jam. Place another slice of dough on top of each and press down lightly to mold dough around filling. Then lightly crimp edges with tines of a fork to seal.

Bake in a 350° oven for 8 to 10 minutes or until lightly browned. Let cool for about 5 minutes on baking sheets, then transfer to racks and let cool completely. Store airtight. Makes about 4 dozen.

Date Pinwheel Cookies

Swirling date filling through a simple brown sugar dough produces a spiral of contrasting color and rich, sweet flavor. Before slicing, be sure to chill the dough thoroughly.

- 1 cup whole pitted dates, snipped
- 2 cups firmly packed brown sugar
- ½ cup water
- ⅔ cup solid vegetable shortening
- 2 eggs
- 1 teaspoon vanilla
- 4 cups all-purpose flour
- 1 teaspoon baking soda
- ¼ teaspoon cream of tartar
- ½ teaspoon salt

In a pan, combine dates, ½ cup of the sugar, and water. Bring to a boil over high heat; then reduce heat and simmer, stirring constantly and mashing with a spoon, until mixture is thick and smooth (about 8 minutes). Remove from heat and let cool completely.

In large bowl of an electric mixer, beat shortening and remaining 1½ cups sugar until creamy; beat in eggs and vanilla. In another bowl, stir together flour, baking soda, cream of tartar, and salt; gradually add to shortening mixture, blending thoroughly to make a stiff dough.

Divide dough in half. Roll out each portion on a floured board, making an 8 by 10-inch rectangle about ¼ inch thick. On each rectangle, spread half the filling to within ½ inch of edges. Then roll up jelly roll style, starting with a long edge. Wrap rolls in wax paper and refrigerate until very firm (at least 12 hours) or for up to 3 days.

Unwrap dough. Using a sharp knife, cut into ¼-inch-thick slices. Place slices slightly apart on ungreased baking sheets. Bake in a 400° oven for 8 to 10 minutes or until lightly browned. Transfer to racks and let cool. Store airtight. Makes about 7 dozen.

Date-Oatmeal Cookies

(Pictured on page 62)

When you bite into these cookies, you'll find a delectable combination of flavors: oats, nuts, dates, and a subtle touch of cinnamon.

  1 **cup (½ lb.) butter or margarine, softened**
  1 **cup sugar**
  1 **teaspoon vanilla**
  2 **eggs**
1¾ **cups all-purpose flour**
  1 **teaspoon** *each* **baking powder and ground cinnamon**
  ¾ **teaspoon baking soda**
  ½ **teaspoon salt**
  2 **cups quick-cooking rolled oats**
  1 **package (8 oz.) whole pitted dates (about 1½ cups lightly packed)**
  1 **cup chopped pecans or walnuts**

In large bowl of an electric mixer, beat butter and sugar until creamy. Beat in vanilla; then beat in eggs, one at a time. In another bowl, stir together flour, baking powder, cinnamon, baking soda, and salt; gradually add to butter mixture, blending thoroughly. Stir in oats, dates, and pecans, mixing well and distributing dates evenly through dough. Shape dough into 2 or 3 rolls, each 1¾ inches in diameter; wrap in wax paper and refrigerate until firm (at least 4 hours) or for up to 3 days.

Unwrap dough. Using a sharp knife, cut into ¼-inch-thick slices; place slices about 1 inch apart on ungreased baking sheets. Bake in a 375° oven for 10 to 12 minutes or until edges are golden. Transfer to racks and let cool. Store airtight. Makes about 6½ dozen.

Peanut Pinwheels

(Pictured on page 62)

In this recipe, a ribbon of chocolate winds its way through the center of a crisp peanut butter cookie.

  ½ **cup (¼ lb.) butter or margarine, softened**
  ½ **cup creamy peanut butter**
  ½ **cup** *each* **granulated sugar and firmly packed brown sugar**
  1 **egg**
1¼ **cups all-purpose flour**
  ½ **teaspoon** *each* **baking soda, salt, and ground cinnamon**
  1 **package (6 oz.) semisweet chocolate chips**

In large bowl of an electric mixer, beat butter, peanut butter, granulated sugar, and brown sugar until creamy; beat in egg. In another bowl, stir together flour, baking soda, salt, and cinnamon; gradually add to butter mixture, blending thoroughly. Cover tightly with plastic wrap and refrigerate until firm (about 2 hours).

In top of a double boiler over simmering water or in a small pan over lowest possible heat, melt chocolate chips, stirring constantly. Let cool slightly. On wax paper, pat chilled dough out into a 12-inch square. Spread chocolate evenly over dough to within ½ inch of edges. Roll up jelly roll style; then cut in half crosswise. Wrap each roll in wax paper and refrigerate until firm (at least 2 hours) or for up to 3 days.

Remove one roll from refrigerator. Unwrap; using a sharp knife, cut into ¼-inch-thick slices. Place slices about 1 inch apart on ungreased baking sheets. Bake in a 375° oven for about 10 minutes or until lightly browned. Let cool on baking sheets for 2 to 3 minutes, then transfer to racks and let cool completely. Repeat with second roll of dough. Store airtight. Makes about 4 dozen.

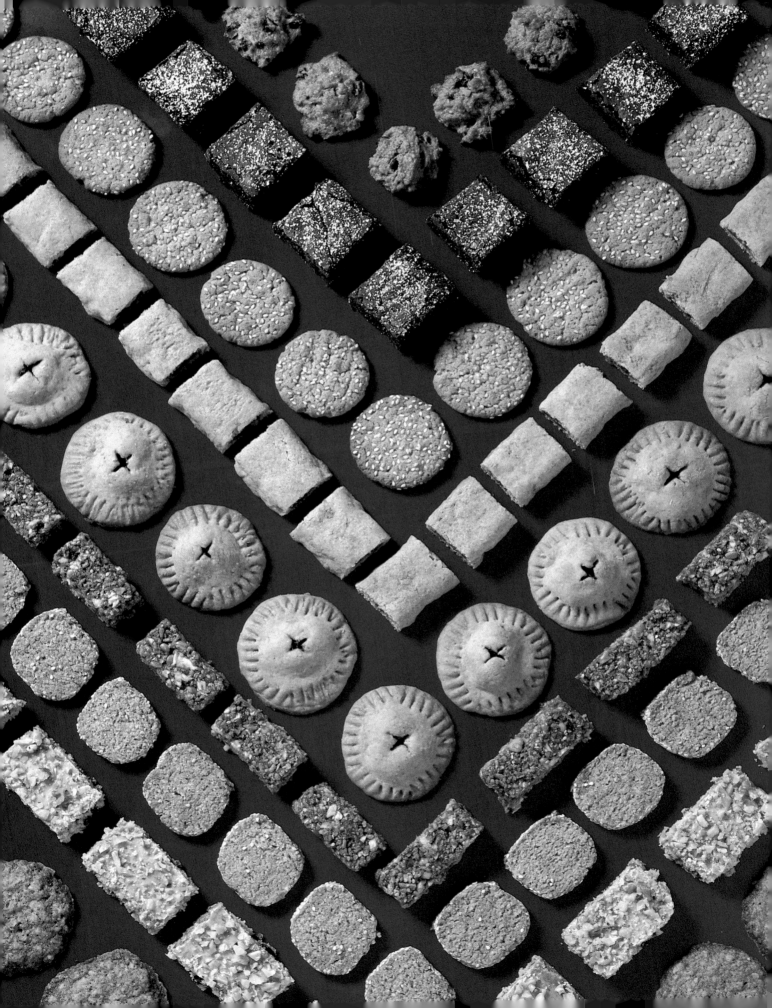

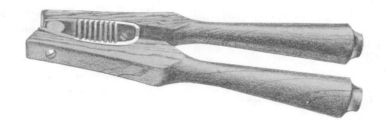

Wholesome Cookies

Cookies that are packed full of nutritious ingredients are the best kind for Scout meetings, school lunches, backpacking, and even for breakfast—especially when they taste wonderful, too. The cookies in this chapter owe their wholesomeness to ingredients such as whole wheat flour, wheat germ, seeds, nuts, dried fruits, and vegetables. Made by the same techniques as other cookies in this book—drop, bar, hand-molded, cut-out, and icebox—they're generally higher in protein, vitamins and minerals, and fiber.

Most of the supplies you'll need to make our wholesome cookies are available in supermarkets, but you may have to visit a health food store for a few ingredients: carob powder, carob chips, granulated fructose, tahini, and unsweetened coconut, for example.

Photo at left reveals a profusion of good-for-you delights. From top to bottom: Half-cup Cookies (page 72), Quick Carob Brownies (page 72), Tahini Cookies (page 73), Fruit Bars (page 79), Date Tarts (page 80), Branapple Bars (page 77), Orange Wheat Cookies (page 76), Zucchini Bars (page 76), and Oatmeal Chews (page 77).

Half-cup Cookies

(Pictured on page 70)

These chunky, down-to-earth drop cookies get their name from the nine (count 'em!) ingredients they include in one-half-cup quantity.

  ½ cup (¼ lb.) butter or margarine, softened
  ½ cup *each* peanut butter and firmly packed brown sugar
  2 eggs
  ½ cup honey
  ¼ cup milk
  ½ teaspoon vanilla
  2 cups whole wheat flour
  1 teaspoon *each* baking powder and ground cinnamon
  ¾ teaspoon salt
  ½ cup *each* semisweet chocolate chips or carob chips; chopped roasted cashews, toasted almonds, or walnut pieces; unsweetened flaked coconut; raisins; and granola-style cereal

In large bowl of an electric mixer, beat butter, peanut butter, and sugar until creamy; beat in eggs, honey, milk, and vanilla. In another bowl, stir together flour, baking powder, cinnamon, and salt; gradually add to butter mixture, blending thoroughly. Mix in chocolate chips, nuts, coconut, raisins, and granola until well combined.

Drop dough by rounded tablespoonfuls onto lightly greased baking sheets, spacing cookies about 1 inch apart. Bake in a 375° oven for about 10 minutes or until golden brown. Transfer to racks and let cool. Store airtight. Makes about 5 dozen.

Carob Chip Cookies

Nutrition-minded cooks favor carob as a substitute for chocolate. Though its flavor, color, and aroma are all reminiscent of light chocolate, carob is lower in fat and contains no caffeine. Both roasted carob powder (see Quick Carob Brownies, following) and carob chips can be used in baking; both are sold in natural food stores and some supermarkets.

These honey-sweetened whole wheat cookies are generously studded with carob chips and sunflower seeds; rolled oats make them chewy (and even more nutritious).

  1 cup solid vegetable shortening
  ½ cup firmly packed brown sugar
  2 eggs
  ¾ cup honey
  1 teaspoon vanilla
  2¼ cups whole wheat flour
  1 teaspoon baking soda
  ¾ teaspoon salt
  ½ cup raw sunflower seeds
  1 cup quick-cooking rolled oats
  8 ounces carob chips (about 1½ cups)

In large bowl of an electric mixer, beat shortening and sugar until creamy; beat in eggs, honey, and vanilla. In another bowl, stir together flour, baking soda, and salt; gradually add to shortening mixture, blending thoroughly. Add sunflower seeds, oats, and carob chips and stir until well combined.

Drop dough by rounded teaspoonfuls onto greased baking sheets, spacing cookies about 2 inches apart. Bake in a 375° oven for about 9 minutes or until golden. Carefully transfer to racks and let cool. Store airtight. Makes about 8 dozen.

Quick Carob Brownies

(Pictured on page 70)

Though it's relatively unfamiliar to many in the United States, carob has been around for a long time. In the Mediterranean area, the carob tree's native environment, carob pods have been a food source for centuries. Carobs also grow in parts of California and Arizona.

When ground and roasted, carob pods yield a brown powder that can be used in baking as a stand-in for unsweetened cocoa—as in these quick-to-mix brownies. Serve the brownies dusted with powdered sugar, or dress them up with a fluffy carob frosting.

  6 tablespoons butter or margarine
  2 eggs
  1 cup granulated sugar
  ½ teaspoon vanilla
  ¾ cup all-purpose flour
  ½ cup roasted carob powder
  1 teaspoon baking powder
  ½ teaspoon salt
    Powdered sugar or Fluffy carob frosting (recipe follows)

Place butter in an 8-inch square baking pan; set pan in oven while oven preheats to 325°. When butter is melted, remove pan from oven and set aside.

In large bowl of an electric mixer, beat eggs, granulated sugar, and vanilla until thick and lemon-colored; pour in butter and stir until blended (set baking pan aside unwashed). In another bowl, stir together flour, carob powder, baking powder, and salt; sift into egg mixture and stir just until smoothly blended.

Spread batter in baking pan and bake in a 325° oven for 25 minutes or until a pick inserted in center comes out clean. Place pan on a rack and let cool completely. Sift powdered sugar lightly over top or prepare fluffy carob frosting and spread on cooled brownies. Cut into 2-inch squares. Store airtight. Makes 16.

Fluffy carob frosting. In small bowl of an electric mixer, lightly beat 1 **egg white.** Add 3 tablespoons **butter** or margarine, softened; a dash of **salt;** ¼ cup **roasted carob powder;** and ¼ teaspoon **vanilla.** Beat until blended. Gradually add 1 cup sifted **powdered sugar,** beating until frosting is smooth and fluffy.

Tahini Cookies

(Pictured on page 70)

The sesame-seed paste called *tahini* is a staple in Middle Eastern cooking, adding rich, nutty flavor to a variety of dishes. Here, we use it in crisp whole wheat cookies topped with toasted sesame seeds.

You'll find tahini in Middle Eastern markets and natural food stores, and also in some well-stocked supermarkets. It keeps almost indefinitely—but, like unhomogenized nut butters, it separates on standing, so stir until smooth and well blended before using.

- ½ cup *each* granulated sugar and firmly packed brown sugar
- ½ cup tahini (stir before measuring)
- 4 tablespoons butter or margarine, softened
- ¼ cup solid vegetable shortening
- 1 egg
- 1⅓ cups whole wheat flour
- ¾ teaspoon baking soda
- ½ teaspoon baking powder
  About 3 tablespoons sesame seeds

In large bowl of an electric mixer, beat granulated sugar, brown sugar, tahini, butter, and shortening until creamy. Beat in egg. In another bowl, stir together flour, baking soda, and baking powder; gradually add to tahini mixture, blending thoroughly. Cover tightly with plastic wrap and refrigerate until easy to handle (about 2 hours) or until next day.

Meanwhile, in a small frying pan over medium heat, toast sesame seeds, shaking pan frequently, until golden (about 2 minutes). Let cool.

Roll dough into 1-inch balls. Dip balls into toasted sesame seeds and press down so seeds adhere to dough; then place balls, seeded side up, about 3 inches apart on ungreased baking sheets. Flatten each ball with a fork dipped in flour, making a crisscross pattern with fork tines.

Bake in a 375° oven for 8 to 10 minutes or until lightly browned. Let cool on baking sheets for 2 minutes; then transfer to racks and let cool completely. Store airtight. Makes about 5 dozen.

Peanut Raisin Honeys

Here's a honey-flavored cookie that makes a good energy-booster on any occasion, from morning coffee to late-night snack.

- 1 cup (½ lb.) butter or margarine, softened
- ½ cup crunchy peanut butter
- 1 cup firmly packed brown sugar
- 2 eggs
- 1 cup honey
- 2 cups *each* whole wheat flour and rolled oats
- 1 cup toasted unsweetened wheat germ
- 1 cup *each* unsweetened flaked coconut, raisins, and chopped salted peanuts

In large bowl of an electric mixer, beat butter, peanut butter, and sugar until creamy. Beat in eggs, one at a time, beating well after each addition, until mixture is fluffy. Mix in honey, flour, oats, and wheat germ, blending thoroughly; add coconut, raisins, and peanuts and mix to distribute evenly.

Drop dough by level tablespoonfuls onto greased baking sheets, spacing cookies about 2 inches apart. Bake in a 375° oven for 10 to 12 minutes or until golden and firm to the touch. Transfer to racks and let cool. Store airtight. Makes about 7 dozen.

Graham Crackers

These crisp, slightly sweet grahams have hearty whole-grain flavor—and they're easy to make. Serve them as is with a glass of milk or a cup of coffee, or top with nutty caramel to make easy graham cracker pralines.

    ¾ cup (¼ lb. plus 4 tablespoons) butter
        or margarine, softened
    ¼ cup honey
    ½ cup firmly packed brown sugar
    1 teaspoon vanilla
    3 cups whole wheat flour
    ½ cup toasted unsweetened wheat germ
    1 teaspoon *each* salt and ground cinnamon
    ½ teaspoon baking powder
    ¾ cup water

In large bowl of an electric mixer, beat butter, honey, brown sugar, and vanilla until creamy. In another bowl, stir together flour, wheat germ, salt, cinnamon, and baking powder. With mixer on low speed, add flour mixture to butter mixture alternately with water, blending well after each addition. Cover tightly with plastic wrap and refrigerate until easy to handle (at least 1 hour) or for up to 3 days.

Divide dough into 2 equal portions; return one portion to refrigerator. On a lightly floured board, pat out other portion into a ½-inch-thick rectangle. Place on a lightly greased unrimmed 12 by 15-inch baking sheet and roll out with a floured rolling pin until dough completely covers baking sheet and is an even ⅛ inch thick. Trim edges with a knife. (If dough becomes too soft, refrigerate again until firm.)

Using a floured pastry wheel or knife, cut dough into 3-inch squares (to obtain straight edges, use a ruler as a guide). Prick each 3 times with a fork. Bake in a 325° oven for about 30 minutes or until very lightly browned; remove crackers around edges of baking sheet if they brown more quickly than center crackers. Transfer crackers to racks and let cool. Repeat with remaining dough. Store airtight. Makes 40.

Cracker Pralines

Place 20 baked **Graham Crackers** close together on a baking sheet; set aside.

In a heavy 1½-quart pan, combine ½ cup firmly packed **brown sugar** and ½ cup (¼ lb.) **butter** or margarine. Bring to a boil over medium heat, stirring constantly. Boil gently (reduce heat if necessary), stirring, for 5 minutes. Remove from heat and stir in ½ cup chopped **walnuts** or almonds, ½ teaspoon **vanilla,** and ¼ teaspoon **ground cinnamon.**

Working quickly, immediately drizzle mixture over crackers and spread evenly with a small spatula. Bake in a 275° oven for 10 minutes, then carefully transfer to racks and let cool. Store airtight. Makes 20.

Nutty Whole Wheat Shortbread
(Pictured on facing page)

The flavor of toasted hazelnuts or almonds makes these whole wheat shortbread cookies almost irresistible. Eat them plain for a sweet snack, or serve alongside a bowl of frozen yogurt or a fruit salad for a nutritious dessert.

    ¾ cup (about ¼ lb.) hazelnuts (filberts)
        or whole blanched almonds
    ½ cup (¼ lb.) butter, softened
    ½ cup sugar
    1 cup whole wheat flour

Spread hazelnuts in a shallow rimmed baking pan and toast in a 350° oven for 10 to 15 minutes or until golden beneath skins; shake pan occasionally. Let cool. (If using almonds, toast for only 8 to 10 minutes.) Pour hazelnuts into a clean dishcloth, fold to enclose, and rub briskly to remove skins. (Omit this step if using almonds.) Whirl nuts in a blender or food processor until finely ground.

In large bowl of an electric mixer, beat butter and sugar until creamy; beat in ground nuts. Gradually add flour, blending thoroughly.

Gather dough into a ball and transfer to a lightly floured board. Roll out to a straight-edged rectangle ¼ inch thick. Cut rectangle lengthwise into thirds; then cut each third into triangles (see photograph on facing page). Or roll out dough free-form, keeping it an even ¼ inch thick, and cut out with cookie cutters (about 2 inches in diameter). Place cookies slightly apart on ungreased baking sheets. Bake in a 350° oven for 10 to 12 minutes or until golden brown. Let cool on baking sheets for 5 minutes, then transfer to racks and let cool completely. Store airtight. Makes about 2 dozen.

Nutty Whole Wheat Shortbread *(Recipe on facing page)*

1 Toast nuts on a rimmed baking sheet until skins have cracked and meat underneath has turned golden.

2 Rub nuts briskly in a towel to remove as much of skins as possible.

3 In a blender or food processor, whirl nuts until finely and evenly ground.

4 Cut rectangle of dough lengthwise into thirds, then cut each third into triangles.

Lemon Carrot Cookies

Shredded carrots add vitamins and natural sweetness to these lemon-flavored drop cookies.

    1   cup (½ lb.) butter or margarine, softened
    ¾   cup sugar
    1   teaspoon lemon extract
    ½   teaspoon vanilla
    1   egg
    1   cup finely shredded carrots
        (about 2 medium-size)
    1   cup *each* all-purpose flour and
        whole wheat flour
    2   teaspoons baking powder
    ¼   teaspoon *each* salt and baking soda
    1½ cups chopped walnuts

In large bowl of an electric mixer, beat butter and sugar until creamy; beat in lemon extract, vanilla, and egg. Stir in carrots. In another bowl, stir together all-purpose flour, whole wheat flour, baking powder, salt, and baking soda; gradually add to butter mixture, blending thoroughly. Mix in walnuts.

Drop dough by level tablespoonfuls onto greased baking sheets, spacing cookies about 2 inches apart. Bake in a 375° oven for 12 minutes or until edges are browned. Transfer to racks and let cool. Store airtight. Makes about 6 dozen.

Orange Wheat Cookies

(Pictured on page 70)

A crunchy, decorative rim of sesame seeds adds interest to these icebox wafers. Daintier than most whole wheat cookies, they have a pleasing crispness and a delicate orange flavor.

    1   cup (½ lb.) butter or margarine, softened
    1   cup firmly packed brown sugar
    1   egg
    1   teaspoon grated orange peel
    2¼ cups whole wheat flour
    1½ cups quick-cooking rolled oats
    ¼   cup sesame seeds

In large bowl of an electric mixer, beat butter and sugar until creamy; beat in egg and orange peel.

Gradually add flour and oats, blending thoroughly. Shape dough into 2 rolls, each about 1½ inches in diameter. Evenly sprinkle 2 tablespoons of the sesame seeds on each of 2 sheets of wax paper. Roll each portion of dough in seeds to coat on all sides; then wrap in wax paper and refrigerate until firm (at least 2 hours) or for up to 3 days.

Unwrap dough. Using a sharp knife, cut into ¼-inch-thick slices; place slices about 1 inch apart on ungreased baking sheets. Bake in a 350° oven for 12 to 15 minutes or until lightly browned. Transfer to racks and let cool. Store airtight. Makes about 5 dozen.

Zucchini Bars

(Pictured on page 70)

Coarse shreds of zucchini, bits of dried fruit, and coconut make these bar cookies extra moist and chewy. They're topped with chopped walnuts for a crunchy finishing touch.

    ¾   cup (¼ lb. plus 4 tablespoons) butter or
        margarine, softened
    ½   cup *each* granulated sugar and firmly
        packed brown sugar
    2   eggs
    2   teaspoons vanilla
    1¾ cups all-purpose flour
    ½   teaspoon salt
    1½ teaspoons baking powder
    ¾   cup *each* unsweetened flaked coconut,
        snipped pitted dates, and raisins
    2   cups unpared, coarsely shredded zucchini
    1   tablespoon butter or margarine, melted
    2   tablespoons milk
    ¼   teaspoon ground cinnamon
    1   cup powdered sugar
    1   cup finely chopped walnuts

In large bowl of an electric mixer, beat the ¾ cup butter, granulated sugar, and brown sugar until creamy; beat in eggs and 1 teaspoon of the vanilla. In another bowl, stir together flour, salt, and baking powder; gradually add to butter mixture, blending thoroughly. Mix in coconut, dates, raisins, and zucchini until well combined.

Spread batter evenly in a greased 10 by 15-inch rimmed baking pan. Bake in a 350° oven for 35 to 40 minutes or until a pick inserted in center comes out clean. Place on a rack and let cool slightly.

In a small bowl, beat together the 1 tablespoon butter, milk, remaining 1 teaspoon vanilla, cinnamon, and powdered sugar. Drizzle glaze over warm cookies, then spread evenly; sprinkle walnuts on top. Let cool completely, then cut into 1½ by 2-inch bars. Store airtight. Makes about 4 dozen.

Oatmeal Chews

(Pictured on page 70)

Oatmeal cookies have long been considered a nutritious snack or lunchbox treat. This delightfully chewy version includes whole wheat flour, chopped walnuts, and wheat germ for a fine toasty flavor that will please children and help nourish them, too.

      1 cup (½ lb.) butter or margarine, softened
      1 cup firmly packed brown sugar
      ¼ cup granulated sugar
      2 eggs
      1 teaspoon vanilla
      1 cup whole wheat flour
      ½ cup toasted unsweetened wheat germ
      1 teaspoon *each* baking soda and
        ground cinnamon
      ½ teaspoon salt
      1½ cups rolled oats
      1 cup chopped walnuts
        Granulated sugar

In large bowl of an electric mixer, beat butter, brown sugar, and the ¼ cup granulated sugar until creamy; beat in eggs and vanilla. In another bowl, stir together flour, wheat germ, baking soda, cinnamon, and salt; gradually add to butter mixture, blending thoroughly. Mix in oats and walnuts. Cover tightly with plastic wrap and refrigerate until easy to handle (about 2 hours) or for up to 3 days.

For each cookie, shape about 1 tablespoon dough into a ball. Place balls about 4 inches apart on well-greased baking sheets. Generously grease the bottom of a glass or jar (one with a wide, flat base). For each cookie, dip glass in granulated sugar; then press ball of dough to flatten it to a thickness of about ¼ inch.

Bake in a 375° oven for 5 to 6 minutes or until lightly browned. Let cool on baking sheets for about a minute, then transfer to racks and let cool completely. Store airtight. Makes about 4½ dozen.

Branapple Bars

(Pictured on page 70)

In recent years, dietary fiber has been recognized as an important component of good nutrition. Perhaps the best source of fiber in our diets is bran—the outer layer of a kernel of wheat (or other grain). Bran is sold in its natural, unprocessed state; it's used in breads and a number of high-fiber breakfast cereals.

These no-bake cookies are made with bran cereal for an extra-high fiber content. Like the "health food candy bars" sold in many markets, they're moist, chewy, and packed with good things—apples, nuts, seeds, peanut butter, and wheat germ, as well as the bran cereal. Served with milk or fruit juice, they make a nutritious snack or breakfast treat.

      1 package (6 oz.) dried apple rings or slices
      3 cups boiling water
      ½ cup sesame seeds
      4 cups whole bran cereal
      ¼ cup toasted unsweetened wheat germ
      ½ cup roasted unsalted sunflower seeds
      ½ cup chopped walnuts or almonds
      1 cup honey
      1½ cups peanut butter
      2 tablespoons butter or margarine
      1 teaspoon ground cinnamon

Place dried apples in a medium-size bowl and pour boiling water over them. Let stand for 20 minutes. Meanwhile, in a wide frying pan over medium heat, toast sesame seeds, shaking pan frequently, until golden (about 2 minutes). Let cool; then place in a large mixing bowl and stir in bran cereal, wheat germ, sunflower seeds, and walnuts. Drain apples well; then whirl in a food processor until finely ground (or put through a food chopper fitted with a fine blade). Add to cereal mixture.

In a 2½ to 3-quart pan, cook honey over medium heat until it reaches 230°F on a candy thermometer; stir in peanut butter, butter, and cinnamon. Cook, stirring, until mixture returns to 230°F. Remove from heat and pour over cereal mixture. Stir with a wooden spoon until thoroughly blended.

Turn mixture into a well-greased 10 by 15-inch rimmed baking pan and press down firmly to fill pan evenly. Cover and refrigerate until firm (about 2 hours); then cut into 2 by 2½-inch bars. Wrap bars individually in foil and store in refrigerator for up to 2 weeks. Makes 2½ dozen.

Fruit Bars *(Recipe on facing page)*

1 Use your fingers and a ruler to form dough into a straight-edged rectangle with square corners.

2 Cut rectangle lengthwise into thirds. Spread dried fruit filling (in this case, prune) evenly down center of each strip.

3 Fold sides over filling to overlap slightly on top. Cut strips in half crosswise and invert onto greased baking sheets.

4 After baking, let cookies cool slightly; then cut each strip into 4 pieces.

Fruit Bars

(Pictured on page 70 and on facing page)

If you like fruit-filled cookies, you'll want to make these moist bars. Our recipe presents a choice of four fruit fillings; use either figs, prunes, apricots, or dates. The cookies keep well, becoming softer and more flavorful after they've stood at least a day.

- ½ cup (¼ lb.) **butter** or margarine, softened
- ½ cup *each* **granulated sugar** and firmly packed **brown sugar**
- 2 **eggs**
- ½ teaspoon **vanilla**
- 1 cup **whole wheat flour**
- 1¼ cups **all-purpose flour**
- ¼ cup **toasted unsweetened wheat germ**
- ¼ teaspoon *each* **salt** and **baking soda**
  Fruit filling (recipes follow)

In large bowl of an electric mixer, beat butter, granulated sugar, and brown sugar until creamy. Beat in eggs and vanilla. In another bowl, stir together whole wheat flour, all-purpose flour, wheat germ, salt, and baking soda; gradually add to butter mixture, blending thoroughly.

Cover dough tightly with plastic wrap and refrigerate until easy to handle (at least 1 hour) or until next day. Meanwhile, prepare fruit filling of your choice; set aside.

Divide dough into 2 equal portions. Return one portion to refrigerator. On a floured board, roll out other portion to a straight-edged 9 by 15-inch rectangle; cut lengthwise into three strips.

Divide cooled fruit filling into 6 equal portions and evenly distribute one portion down center of each strip, bringing it out to ends. Use a long spatula to lift sides of each dough strip over filling, overlapping edges slightly on top. Press together lightly. Cut strips in half crosswise; lift and invert onto greased baking sheets (seam side should be down). Brush off excess flour. Refrigerate for about 15 minutes. Meanwhile, repeat rolling and filling with remaining dough.

Bake in a 375° oven for 15 to 20 minutes or until browned. Let cool on baking sheets on a rack for about 10 minutes; then cut each strip crosswise into 4 pieces. Transfer cookies to racks and let cool completely. Store covered. Makes 4 dozen.

Fig filling. Using a food processor or a food chopper fitted with a medium blade, grind together 1 pound **dried figs** (about 2 cups lightly packed) and ½ cup **walnuts** or almonds. Turn into a medium-size pan and add ⅓ cup **sugar,** ½ cup **water,** 1 teaspoon grated **lemon peel,** and 2 tablespoons **lemon juice.** Place over medium heat and cook, stirring, until mixture boils and becomes very thick (5 to 8 minutes). Let cool completely.

Prune filling. Follow directions for **Fig filling,** but substitute 2 cups lightly packed **moist-pack pitted prunes** for figs and add ¾ teaspoon **ground cinnamon** with sugar.

Apricot filling. Follow directions for **Fig filling,** but substitute 3 cups lightly packed **dried apricots** for figs and use 1 teaspoon grated **orange peel** in place of lemon peel.

Date filling. Follow directions for **Fig filling,** but substitute 1 pound **pitted dates** for figs and increase lemon peel to 2 teaspoons.

Chewy Granola Brownies

Not all brownies are dark and chocolaty, as this version proves. Its golden color and rich flavor come from brown sugar and crunchy granola-style cereal.

- ½ cup (¼ lb.) **butter** or margarine
- 1¾ cups firmly packed **brown sugar**
- 2 **eggs,** lightly beaten
- 1 teaspoon **vanilla**
- ¾ cup *each* **all-purpose flour** and **whole wheat flour**
- 2 teaspoons **baking powder**
- ¾ teaspoon **salt**
- 1½ cups **granola-style cereal** (break up any large lumps before measuring)
- ½ cup chopped **nuts** (optional)

Melt butter in a medium-size pan over medium heat. Remove from heat and mix in sugar. Stir in eggs and vanilla; set aside.

In a mixing bowl, stir together all-purpose flour, whole wheat flour, baking powder, and salt. Add sugar mixture and stir until well combined. Stir in granola, then nuts (if used). Spread batter in a greased 9 by 13-inch baking pan.

Bake in a 350° oven for 25 minutes or until a pick inserted in center comes out clean (do not overbake). Let cool in pan on a rack, then cut into 1½ by 3-inch bars. Store airtight. Makes about 2 dozen.

Date Tarts

(Pictured on page 70)

Dates have a history of cultivation that goes back 4,500 years, to the Middle East and North Africa. In these regions, the fruit was so important a food source that it was known as "bread of the desert." Though dates taste as sugary-sweet as candy, they're quite nutritious, containing relatively large amounts of potassium, iron, and niacin, as well as some protein and fiber.

Here, the sun-ripened fruits lend their rich flavor and wholesomeness to a fancy filled cookie. We've called it a "date tart" because of its resemblance to a plump little pie.

> ½ cup (¼ lb.) butter or margarine, softened
> 1 cup firmly packed brown sugar
> 2 eggs
> 1 teaspoon vanilla
> 2 cups all-purpose flour
> ½ cup toasted unsweetened wheat germ
> ½ teaspoon *each* salt and ground nutmeg
> ¼ teaspoon baking soda
> Date filling (recipe follows)

In large bowl of an electric mixer, beat butter and sugar until creamy; beat in eggs and vanilla. In another bowl, stir together flour, wheat germ, salt, nutmeg, and baking soda; gradually add to butter mixture, blending thoroughly. Cover dough tightly with plastic wrap and refrigerate until easy to handle (at least 2 hours) or for up to 3 days. Meanwhile, prepare date filling.

Take out a third of the dough, leaving remaining dough in refrigerator. On a well-floured board, roll out dough to a thickness of ⅟₁₆ inch; cut out with a 3-inch round cookie cutter. Repeat with remaining dough, rolling and cutting one portion at a time.

Place half the cookies slightly apart on greased baking sheets; spoon a heaping teaspoonful of filling onto each. Cover each with another cookie and press edges together with a floured fork. Decoratively slash top, if desired. Bake in a 350° oven for 12 to 15 minutes or until lightly browned. Transfer to racks and let cool. Store airtight. Makes about 2½ dozen.

Date filling. In a small pan, combine 1½ cups lightly packed **pitted dates,** ½ cup **water,** and 2 tablespoons **honey.** Cook over medium heat, stirring and mashing with a spoon, until mixture is thick and smooth. Stir in ½ teaspoon **vanilla.** Let cool; then cover and refrigerate.

Apricot Bran Chews

Breakfast from a cookie jar? Why not, when the cookies are as wholesome as these. Paired with a glass of milk, they offer quick, easily handled nourishment to start the day—a boon to those whose schedules demand on-the-go meals.

> ⅓ cup whole bran cereal
> ¼ cup water
> ¾ cup (¼ lb. plus 4 tablespoons) butter or margarine, softened
> ¼ cup firmly packed brown sugar
> 1 egg
> ¼ cup honey
> 1 teaspoon vanilla
> 1 cup all-purpose flour
> 1 teaspoon baking powder
> ¼ teaspoon *each* salt and baking soda
> ¼ cup instant nonfat dry milk
> 1 cup rolled oats
> ¾ cup chopped walnuts
> 1 cup finely chopped dried apricots

Combine bran cereal and water in a small bowl; set aside. In large bowl of an electric mixer, beat butter and sugar until creamy; add egg and beat until fluffy. Mix in honey, vanilla, and cereal mixture. In another bowl, stir together flour, baking powder, salt, baking soda, dry milk, oats, walnuts, and apricots; gradually add to butter mixture, blending thoroughly.

Drop dough by level tablespoonfuls onto greased baking sheets, spacing cookies about 2 inches apart. Bake in a 375° oven for 10 minutes or until golden brown and firm to the touch. Transfer to racks and let cool. Store airtight. Makes 3 to 4 dozen.

Fructose Spice Cookies

All of us are familiar with sucrose—ordinary table sugar. But fructose, a sugar found in many fruits and vegetables, is becoming increasingly available in supermarkets and natural food stores. Sold in granulated form, it looks and tastes like sucrose, but it's up to 1½ times sweeter, depending on how it's used. You can often use less fructose than sucrose for the same degree of sweetness.

Baked goods made with fructose are moister and brown more readily than those made with sucrose. If you'd like to try baking with fructose, it's best to use recipes specifically designed for it—such as this one, for soft, chewy spice cookies.

- 1 **cup granulated fructose**
- ½ **cup (¼ lb.) butter or margarine, melted**
- 2 **eggs, lightly beaten**
- 1 **teaspoon grated lemon peel**
- 2 **teaspoons vanilla**
- 1 **cup** *each* **all-purpose flour and whole wheat flour**
- 1 **teaspoon cream of tartar**
- ½ **teaspoon baking soda**
- 1½ **teaspoons ground cinnamon**
- ¼ **teaspoon** *each* **ground nutmeg and salt**
- ⅛ **teaspoon ground cloves**

In a large bowl, stir together fructose and butter; mix in eggs, lemon peel, and vanilla. In another bowl, stir together all-purpose flour, whole wheat flour, cream of tartar, baking soda, cinnamon, nutmeg, salt, and cloves; add to egg mixture and stir until blended. Cover dough tightly with plastic wrap and refrigerate until firm (about 2 hours).

Force dough through a cookie press to form round shapes, spacing cookies about 1½ inches apart on greased baking sheets. (Or drop rounded teaspoonfuls of dough 1½ inches apart.) Bake in a 350° oven for 10 to 12 minutes or until firm to the touch. Transfer to racks and let cool. Store airtight. Makes 4 to 5 dozen.

Tutti Frutti Oat Bars

Apple juice and three kinds of dried fruit—raisins, apricots, and dates—go into the filling for these oat-topped treats.

- **Fruit filling (recipe follows)**
- ½ **cup (¼ lb.) butter or margarine, softened**
- 1 **cup firmly packed brown sugar**
- 1½ **cups all-purpose flour**
- ½ **teaspoon** *each* **baking soda and salt**
- 1½ **cups rolled oats**
- 2 **tablespoons water**

Prepare fruit filling; set aside.

In large bowl of an electric mixer, beat butter and sugar until creamy. In another bowl, stir

together flour, baking soda, and salt; gradually add to butter mixture, blending thoroughly. Add oats and water and mix until well combined and crumbly.

Pat half the crumb mixture firmly into a greased 9 by 13-inch baking pan. Spread with cooled fruit filling. Spoon remaining crumb mixture evenly over filling; pat down firmly. Bake in a 350° oven for about 35 minutes or until lightly browned. Let cool in pan on a rack, then cut into 1½ by 2½-inch bars. Store covered. Makes about 2½ dozen.

Fruit filling. In a small pan, combine ¼ cup **sugar** and 1 tablespoon **cornstarch**. Stir in 1 cup **unsweetened apple juice**, 1 teaspoon grated **lemon peel**, 1 tablespoon **lemon juice**, 1 cup **raisins**, and ½ cup *each* finely chopped, lightly packed **dried apricots** and lightly packed snipped **pitted dates**. Cook over medium heat, stirring, until mixture boils and thickens; let cool.

Lunchbox Cookies

Freshly baked cookies make an excellent addition to a lunchbox, adding a little touch of home to a meal eaten elsewhere. When deciding on cookies to tuck into someone's lunch, choose ones that are sturdy enough to pack and carry well. Here are a dozen suggestions; for more, see "Which Cookies to Send," page 17.

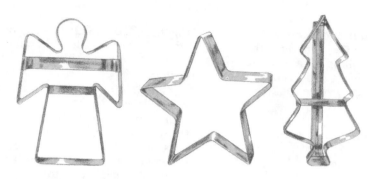

Holiday Cookies

Holidays and cookies go together naturally—festive occasions just seem to call for a bite of something sweet. Christmas, of course, is the holiday most often associated with baking, but Valentine's Day and Halloween are often celebrated with special cookies of their own.

The Christmas cookies in this chapter include a number of traditional favorites, such as Gingerbread Boys (page 92), Nürnberger Lebkuchen (page 92), and Speculaas (page 93). In addition, we present recipes for some really unusual holiday treats: cookie ornaments with candy centers that resemble stained glass, almond cookies that you shape into little partridges and pears, and a gingerbread log cabin that would make a show-stopping buffet centerpiece.

Many of the cookies in this chapter are good gift candidates; some of the Christmas cookies can also be hung on a tree or tied with ribbons to gift packages.

Photo at right celebrates three holidays with a fanfare of festive cookies. In center: Kiss-me Cookies (page 84). In corners: Halloween Cookie Pops (page 87). Others, from top to bottom: Fruitcake Cookie Cups (page 87); Candy Cane Crisps (page 90); Nürnberger Lebkuchen (page 92); Glazed Mincemeat Drops (page 89); Speculaas (page 93); Glazed Mincemeat Drops; Nürnberger Lebkuchen; Candy Cane Crisps; and Fruitcake Cookie Cups.

Valentine's Day

What better way to say "Happy Valentine's Day" than with a gift of freshly baked cookies? Whether you're expressing your affection for the gang at the office, some very special children, or your one and only, cookies make a declaration of love that Cupid himself couldn't resist.

Kiss-me Cookies

(Pictured on page 83)

Vendors at German festivals sell big, spicy cookie hearts, decorated with sentimental messages written in icing. The hearts are tied onto ribbons so they can be worn as badges of affection—many a hopeful lad has draped one about the neck of a pretty Fräulein.

To make these hearts at home, you start with a traditional lebkuchen dough, cutting it into large hearts with the aid of a paper pattern; use purchased icing to inscribe your message. Any language will do, but these German phrases are most authentic: *Liebling* (darling), *Mein Schatz* (my treasure), *Küss mich* (kiss me), *Du bist mein Alles* (you are my everything), *Alte Liebe rostet nicht* (old love never rusts), *Nur du* (only you), *Du bist mein Traum* (you are my dream), *Ich liebe dich* (I love you), *Liebst du mich?* (do you love me?), *Bist du mein?* (are you mine?), *Heute oder nie* (today or never), *Bleib mir treu* (stay true to me).

- ¾ cup honey
- ⅔ cup firmly packed brown sugar
- 1 teaspoon grated lemon peel
- 4 tablespoons butter or margarine
- 2 eggs
- 3¾ cups all-purpose flour
- ½ teaspoon baking soda
- ¼ teaspoon salt
- ½ cup almonds, ground
- 1 teaspoon ground ginger
- ½ teaspoon ground cinnamon
- ¼ teaspoon ground nutmeg
- ½ cup minced candied orange peel
- 1 egg yolk beaten with 1 tablespoon water
  Purchased decorating icing (in tubes or aerosol cans)

In a small pan, combine honey, sugar, lemon peel, and butter; stir over medium heat until butter is melted. Let cool to lukewarm. In a large mixing bowl, beat eggs until foamy; stir in honey mixture. In another bowl, stir together flour, baking soda, salt, almonds, ginger, cinnamon, nutmeg, and orange peel; gradually add to egg mixture, blending thoroughly.

To make cookie pattern, cut as large a heart shape as possible from a 7 by 8-inch rectangle of heavy paper. Divide dough into 8 equal portions; dust with flour and shake off excess. On a lightly floured board, roll out one portion of dough until just slightly larger than pattern. Transfer dough to a greased baking sheet and place pattern on top; cut around pattern with a knife and remove scraps.

Repeat with remaining dough, spacing cookies slightly apart on baking sheets. Combine scraps and re-roll to make 1 or 2 additional hearts. Brush cookies with egg yolk mixture. Bake in a 350° oven for 12 to 15 minutes or until lightly browned. Transfer to racks and let cool completely.

Decorate cookies with icing, making a decorative border around edges and writing messages in center (white icing and a plain tip are best for writing). Let dry, uncovered, until icing is firm (several hours or until next day). Wrap each cookie snugly in plastic wrap, joining overlaps on back (tape, if necessary). With an ice pick or metal skewer, make 2 evenly spaced holes near the top of each heart; then force a piece of narrow ribbon through plastic and cookie. Tie ribbon ends, making loop long enough to fit over a head. Store airtight for up to 2 weeks. Makes 8 to 10.

Raspberry-Nut Valentines

(Pictured on front cover)

Rich, European-style nut cookies cut into heart shapes are the foundation for these fancy jam-filled sandwiches. A shower of powdered sugar provides a pastry-shop finish.

- 1 cup (½ lb.) butter or margarine, softened
- ⅔ cup granulated sugar
- ½ teaspoon vanilla
- 1⅓ cups pecans, ground
- 2 cups all-purpose flour
  Powdered sugar
  About ¼ cup raspberry jam

In large bowl of an electric mixer, beat butter and granulated sugar until creamy; beat in vanilla. Gradually add pecans and flour, blending thoroughly. Cover tightly with plastic wrap and refrigerate until easy to handle (1 to 2 hours) or for up to 3 days.

On a floured board, roll out dough to a thickness of ⅛ inch. Cut out with a 2-inch heart-shaped cookie cutter and transfer to ungreased baking sheets, spacing about 1 inch apart. Cut out a hole in center of half of the cookies, using a tiny round cutter about ½ inch in diameter (you can use the cap from a vanilla or other extract bottle). Bake in a 375° oven for about 12 minutes or until lightly browned. Transfer to racks and let cool completely.

Sift powdered sugar over tops of cookies with holes; then spread bottom sides of remaining cookies with jam. Place a sugar-topped cookie on each jam-topped cookie to form a sandwich. Store airtight. Makes about 3 dozen.

Lemon Hearts

"Sweets for the sweet" is an appropriate announcement on February 14, when you present your valentine with a basketful of these crisp, buttery lemon cookies. Each is sprinkled with sugar before baking and crowned with half a candied cherry.

> 1 cup (½ lb.) butter or margarine, softened
> 1 cup sugar
> 1 egg yolk
> 3 teaspoons grated lemon peel
> 2 cups all-purpose flour
> ½ cup ground blanched almonds
>   Sugar
>   About 20 candied cherries, cut in half

In large bowl of an electric mixer, beat butter and the 1 cup sugar until creamy; beat in egg yolk and lemon peel. Gradually add flour, blending thoroughly; stir in almonds. Gather dough into a ball with your hands.

On a lightly floured board, roll out dough to a thickness of ¼ inch. Cut out with a 2 to 3-inch heart-shaped cookie cutter; transfer cookies to greased baking sheets, spacing about 1 inch apart. Sprinkle cookies lightly with sugar. Place half a cherry, cut side down, in center of each and press in lightly.

Bake in a 325° oven for about 20 minutes or until edges are golden. Transfer to racks and let cool completely. Store airtight. Makes about 3½ dozen.

Halloween

When the wind whistles, the back door creaks, and you seem to hear an owl hooting in the distance, ward off the witches with these delicious Halloween cookies.

Pumpkin Bars

These pumpkin spice bars are ideal for Halloween parties; you might also serve them at Thanksgiving as an alternative to pumpkin pie.

> 4 eggs
> ¾ cup salad oil
> 2 cups sugar
> 1 can (about 15 oz.) pumpkin
> 2 cups all-purpose flour
> 2 teaspoons ground cinnamon
> ¾ teaspoon *each* ground ginger, cloves, and nutmeg
> ¾ teaspoon salt
> 2 teaspoons baking powder
> 1 teaspoon baking soda
>   Orange cream cheese frosting (recipe follows)
>   About 72 whole unblanched almonds (optional)

In large bowl of an electric mixer, beat eggs lightly; beat in oil, sugar, and pumpkin. In another bowl, stir together flour, cinnamon, ginger, cloves, nutmeg, salt, baking powder, and baking soda; gradually add to pumpkin mixture, blending thoroughly.

Pour batter into a greased and flour-dusted 10 by 15-inch rimmed baking pan. Bake in a 350° oven for about 35 minutes or until edges begin to pull away from pan sides and center springs back when lightly touched. Let cool in pan on a rack. Prepare orange cream cheese frosting and spread over cooled cookies; cut into 1 by 2-inch bars. If desired, top each bar with an almond. Store covered. Makes about 6 dozen.

Orange cream cheese frosting. In small bowl of an electric mixer, beat 1 small package (3 oz.) **cream cheese** (softened) and 2 tablespoons **butter** or margarine (softened) until fluffy. Beat in 1½ teaspoons **milk,** ½ teaspoon **vanilla,** and ¾ teaspoon grated **orange peel.** Gradually sift in enough **powdered sugar** (about 2 cups) to make a spreadable icing.

Halloween Cookie Pops *(Recipe on facing page)*

1 Lay homemade patterns on rolled-out dough; cut around patterns with a small, sharp knife.

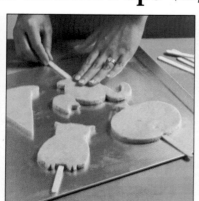

2 Gently insert sticks 1½ to 2 inches into base of each cookie before baking. If dough is too soft, cover and refrigerate briefly.

3 Tint icing as desired; spread over each baked and cooled cookie.

4 Add decorations before icing sets; let children choose from an assortment of colored candies.

Halloween Cookie Pops

(Pictured on facing page and on page 83)

These delightful cookies-on-sticks make fine Halloween treats for your favorite little goblins.

- ⅔ **cup solid vegetable shortening**
- ⅔ **cup butter or margarine, softened**
- ¾ **cup** *each* **granulated sugar and firmly packed brown sugar**
- 2 **eggs**
- 2 **teaspoons vanilla**
- 3½ **cups all-purpose flour**
- 2 **teaspoons baking powder**
- 1 **teaspoon salt**
- 4 **teaspoons pumpkin pie spice or 1 teaspoon** *each* **ground allspice, cinnamon, ginger, and nutmeg**
- **Confectioner's icing (recipe follows)**
- **Assorted candy decorations**

In large bowl of an electric mixer, beat shortening, butter, granulated sugar, and brown sugar until creamy; beat in eggs and vanilla. In another bowl, stir together flour, baking powder, salt, and pumpkin pie spice; gradually add to butter mixture, blending thoroughly. Cover tightly with plastic wrap and refrigerate for 1 to 2 hours.

Meanwhile, cut cookie patterns from lightweight cardboard, choosing simple Halloween shapes and making them 5 to 6 inches wide at the widest point. Also have ready 4½ to 5½-inch Popsicle sticks or tongue depressors.

Using a stockinet-covered or floured rolling pin, roll out dough, a portion at a time, on a floured board to a thickness of about ⅜ inch. (Keep remaining dough refrigerated until ready to roll.) Place patterns on dough and cut around edges with a knife. Remove patterns; use a wide spatula to transfer cookies carefully to ungreased baking sheets, spacing them about 2 inches apart. Insert Popsicle sticks 1½ to 2 inches into the base of each.

Bake in a 375° oven for 12 to 15 minutes or until very lightly browned. Transfer to racks and let cool completely. Prepare confectioner's icing and spread on cooled cookies; decorate with candies as desired. Let icing dry thoroughly, then wrap cookies individually in plastic wrap. Store in a single layer on a flat surface. Makes about 1 dozen.

Confectioner's icing. In a bowl, stir together 2 cups sifted **powdered sugar** and enough **milk** (about 3 tablespoons) to make a spreadable icing. Tint with **food color** as desired.

Christmas

Christmas is the time when many home bakers like to display their talents, producing batch after batch of festive cookies to delight family and friends. Our Christmas cookie collection includes some familiar old standbys and some new ideas; elsewhere in this book, you'll find more treats for your holiday cookie tray—try Norwegian Kringle, page 37; Finnish Ribbon Cakes, page 39; Italian Fruit Cookies, page 41; Swedish Ginger Thins, page 49; Spritz, page 55; Almond Ravioli Cookies, page 57; and Mint Meringues, page 16.

Fruitcake Cookie Cups

(Pictured on pages 83 and 94)

Like miniature Christmas fruitcakes, these moist cookies age well. You bake them in little paper bonbon cups, available in cookware shops.

- 4 **tablespoons butter or margarine, softened**
- ½ **cup firmly packed brown sugar**
- ¼ **cup apple or red currant jelly**
- 2 **eggs**
- 1 **teaspoon vanilla**
- 1½ **cups all-purpose flour**
- 2 **teaspoons baking soda**
- ½ **teaspoon** *each* **ground allspice, cloves, cinnamon, and nutmeg**
- 1 **cup chopped walnuts or pecans**
- 1 **cup currants or raisins**
- 1 **cup chopped candied cherries or mixed candied fruit**

In large bowl of an electric mixer, beat butter and sugar until creamy; beat in jelly, eggs, and vanilla. In another bowl, stir together flour, baking soda, allspice, cloves, cinnamon, and nutmeg. Blend half the flour mixture into butter mixture. Add walnuts, currants, and cherries to remaining flour mixture; then stir into butter mixture, blending thoroughly.

Spoon 1½ to 2 teaspoons batter into each paper bonbon cup and place about 1 inch apart on baking sheets; or drop batter by rounded teaspoonfuls directly onto lightly greased baking sheets, spacing cookies about 2 inches apart. Bake in a 300° oven for 17 to 20 minutes or until centers spring back when lightly touched. Let cool on racks. Store airtight. Makes about 6 dozen.

Partridge & Pear Cookies

Three French hens, two turtle doves—any child could complete the line, especially if he or she saw your tree decorated with partridges and pears made of almond cookie dough. Whole cloves provide stems for the pears, eyes for the birds, and hangers for both; a lightly tinted egg white glaze lends a blush of color.

>   1 cup (½ lb.) butter or margarine, softened
>   8 ounces almond paste
>   ¾ cup sugar
>   1 egg
>   3 cups all-purpose flour
>   Whole cloves
>   Egg white glaze (recipe follows)

In large bowl of an electric mixer, beat butter, almond paste, and sugar until creamy; beat in egg. Gradually add flour, blending thoroughly.

Shape just a few cookies at a time, keeping remaining dough covered. For each cookie, use about 2 tablespoons of dough; flatten and shape into a partridge or pear. Insert cloves and prick partridge cookies as shown in illustrations below. Transfer cookies to ungreased baking sheets, spacing about 1 inch apart.

Bake in a 325° oven for about 20 minutes or until lightly browned on bottoms. Transfer to racks and let cool. Prepare egg white glaze; use a watercolor brush or soft pastry brush to apply a thin wash of color to cookies. Store airtight. Makes about 3½ dozen.

Egg white glaze. Beat 1 **egg white** until frothy; beat in ½ cup sifted **powdered sugar.** Divide glaze into portions and tint lightly with yellow, red, and/or orange **food color.**

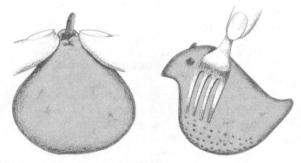

For stem of pear, insert bud end of clove; shape and press dough firmly around it. Partridge has clove hanger and eye; prick with a fork to simulate speckled breast.

Stained-glass Cookies

(Pictured on page 94)

Shimmering red or green candy centers accent these crisp cut-out cookies. Each one has a loop of ribbon attached, so you can hang them on your Christmas tree or tie them to gifts as edible decorations. The cookies are made from a sour cream dough flavored with nutmeg—but if you prefer, you can substitute the dough used for our Gingerbread Log Cabin (page 90).

For shaping, you'll need a 4-inch round cookie cutter (or a tuna can with ends removed) and some smaller cutters for making the center cutouts. Also have ready about 7½ yards of ¼-inch ribbon for hanging.

Though these ornaments are quite durable, their candy centers may run if you hang them near a hot light or where humidity is high. To prevent this, we recommend heat-sealing the cookies in plastic wrap (directions follow).

>   ½ cup (¼ lb.) butter or margarine, softened
>   ½ cup solid vegetable shortening
>   1½ cups sugar
>   ½ cup sour cream
>   1 teaspoon vanilla
>   1 egg
>   3¾ cups all-purpose flour
>   1 teaspoon ground nutmeg
>   ½ teaspoon *each* baking soda and salt
>   2 cups sugar
>   1 cup light corn syrup
>   ½ cup water
>   Red or green food color
>   ½ to 1 teaspoon flavoring, such as raspberry, peppermint, or pineapple

In large bowl of an electric mixer, beat butter, shortening, and the 1½ cups sugar until creamy; beat in sour cream, vanilla, and egg. In another bowl, stir together flour, nutmeg, baking soda, and salt; gradually add to butter mixture, blending thoroughly. Cover dough tightly with plastic wrap and refrigerate until next day.

Divide dough into quarters. Work with one portion at a time; keep remaining dough refrigerated until ready to roll. Roll out on a floured board to a thickness of ⅛ inch. Cut out with a 4-inch round cookie cutter and transfer to greased baking sheets, spacing cookies about 1 inch apart. Refrigerate sheets. When cookies are cold, cut out centers with a smaller cutter. Refrigerate scraps to re-roll with remaining dough.

Bake cookies in a 375° oven for 6 to 7 minutes or just until firm but not yet browned around edges. Let cool on baking sheets for 5 minutes; transfer to a flat surface and let cool completely.

Cut ¼-inch ribbon into 8-inch lengths. Loop a piece of ribbon through center of each cooled cookie; tie securely at top. Arrange cookies, right side up, on greased baking sheets.

For candy centers, place two 1-cup glass measuring cups in a 375° oven to preheat. Combine the 2 cups sugar, corn syrup, and water in a 2-quart pan. Cook over medium-high heat, stirring, until sugar is dissolved. Then cook without stirring until syrup reaches 280°F (hard crack stage) on a candy thermometer. Remove from heat; stir in your choice of food color and flavoring.

Remove one measuring cup from oven; fill with half the syrup (keep remaining syrup over low heat). As soon as syrup in cup stops bubbling, hold cup with a potholder and pour syrup in a thin stream to fill cookie centers. Repeat, using second cup and remaining syrup. Let cookies cool completely; twist gently to loosen, then slide off sheets. Store airtight in a single layer in a cool, dry place, or heat-seal in plastic wrap (see below). Makes about 2½ dozen.

To heat-seal, lay a piece of brown paper (or a piece of paper bag) on a baking sheet. Set sheet in oven and heat to 300°. Tear plastic wrap into 8-inch lengths. Wrap each cookie; secure with cellophane tape. Place about 4 cookies at a time, right sides up, on paper; close oven door for 20 seconds. Remove and let cool.

Brandy Balls

The flavor of brandy enlivens these rich and nutty holiday nuggets.

- 1¼ cups (½ lb. plus 4 tablespoons) butter or margarine, softened
- ½ cup granulated sugar
- 1 egg yolk
- 2 teaspoons brandy flavoring
- 3 cups all-purpose flour
- ¼ teaspoon salt
- 1 cup finely chopped pecans or walnuts
  Powdered sugar

In large bowl of an electric mixer, beat butter and granulated sugar until creamy; beat in egg yolk and brandy flavoring. In another bowl, stir to-

gether flour and salt; gradually add to butter mixture, blending thoroughly. Stir in pecans until well combined.

Roll dough into 1-inch balls and place about 1 inch apart on lightly greased baking sheets. Bake in a 350° oven for about 25 minutes or until firm to the touch and very light golden. Transfer to racks and let cool slightly; while still warm, roll in powdered sugar to coat. Let cool completely. Store airtight. Makes about 4 dozen.

Glazed Mincemeat Drops

(Pictured on page 83)

Old-fashioned mincemeat recipes usually call for beef and suet. These holiday drop cookies are made with purchased mincemeat, which contains mainly fruit and sweeteners with little or no meat—but they still boast traditional spicy flavor and festive seasonal appeal.

- 1 cup (½ lb.) butter or margarine, softened
- 1½ cups firmly packed brown sugar
- 3 eggs
- 3 cups all-purpose flour
- ½ teaspoon *each* baking powder and salt
- 1 teaspoon *each* baking soda and ground cinnamon
- 1 cup rolled oats
- 2 cups prepared mincemeat
- 1 cup chopped walnuts
  Spicy glaze (recipe follows)

In large bowl of an electric mixer, beat butter and sugar until creamy; beat in eggs. In another bowl, stir together flour, baking powder, salt, baking soda, cinnamon, and oats. Gradually add to butter mixture, blending thoroughly. Stir in mincemeat and walnuts.

Drop dough by level tablespoonfuls onto greased baking sheets, spacing cookies 3 inches apart. Bake in a 400° oven for 8 to 10 minutes or until golden brown.

Transfer cookies to racks. Prepare spicy glaze and spread over tops of cookies while they're still warm; let cool completely. Store airtight. Makes 6 to 7 dozen.

Spicy glaze. In a bowl, stir together 3 cups **powdered sugar,** ¾ teaspoon **ground cinnamon,** and 3 tablespoons *each* **brandy** and **water** (or 6 tablespoons water) until smooth.

Gingerbread Log Cabin

(Pictured on facing page)

This sugary, snow-covered log cabin is easily assembled from gingerbread "logs" cut out with homemade cardboard patterns; you'll also need a 12-inch square of stiff cardboard for a "foundation." Complete the edible winter wonderland with decorative details cut from leftover dough. Or use your favorite holiday decorations—tiny Christmas trees, figurines, toy reindeer, and the like.

    ¾ cup solid vegetable shortening
    ¾ cup granulated sugar
    ¾ cup molasses
    2 tablespoons water
    3¼ cups all-purpose flour
    1 teaspoon *each* salt, baking soda, and
      ground ginger
    ¼ teaspoon *each* ground nutmeg and allspice
      Icing (recipe follows)
      About 4 cups powdered sugar

In large bowl of an electric mixer, beat shortening and granulated sugar until creamy; beat in molasses and water. In another bowl, stir together flour, salt, baking soda, ginger, nutmeg, and allspice; gradually add to shortening mixture, blending thoroughly. Cover tightly with plastic wrap and refrigerate until firm (about 2 hours).

Meanwhile, prepare foundation for cabin by covering a 12-inch square of stiff cardboard with foil. Also prepare patterns for cutting logs: cut lightweight cardboard into a 4 by 6-inch rectangle (for the roof); ½-inch-wide strips that are 2, 3½, and 6 inches long (for logs); and a ½-inch square (for spacers).

With a floured rolling pin, roll out a third of the dough on a floured board to a thickness of ⅛ inch (keep remaining dough refrigerated). Make 2 roof sections by cutting around roof pattern with a sharp knife; transfer carefully to a lightly greased baking sheet.

Roll out scraps and all remaining dough to a thickness of ⅜ inch. Then cut out eight 2-inch-long logs, two 3½-inch-long logs, seventeen 6-inch-long logs, and 30 spacers (½-inch squares). Transfer cookies to lightly greased baking sheets (bake separately from roof sections), arranging about 1 inch apart. From remaining dough, cut out trees or other decorative details. Extra spacers can be used for chimney and stepping stones.

Bake in a 350° oven for 12 to 15 minutes or until just firm to the touch (cookies will harden as they cool). As soon as roof section is baked, lay pattern on each section and evenly trim one long edge (where the 2 sections will meet). Let cookies cool briefly on baking sheets, then transfer to racks and let cool completely. If not assembling cabin at once, package airtight; freeze if desired.

Prepare icing. With a pastry brush, paint foil-covered foundation with icing, then sift some of the powdered sugar over icing to cover lightly. Assemble cabin, following steps 1 through 4 at right and using icing as glue wherever logs join. Decorate as desired with extra shapes.

In most dry climates, cabin will keep for about 1 week. In humid areas, cookies may absorb moisture and start to sag, so plan to keep cabin for only 2 or 3 days before eating.

Icing. In a bowl, beat together 2 cups **powdered sugar** and ¼ cup **water** until smooth.

Candy Cane Crisps

(Pictured on page 83)

The month of December is punctuated with occasions calling for cookies, and these crisp morsels suit the season perfectly.

    1 cup (½ lb.) butter or margarine, softened
      About 1¼ cups powdered sugar
    1½ teaspoons vanilla
    1⅓ cups all-purpose flour
    1 cup rolled oats
    ½ teaspoon salt
      About ¾ cup coarsely crushed candy canes

In large bowl of an electric mixer, beat butter and 1 cup of the sugar until creamy; beat in vanilla. In another bowl, stir together flour, oats, and salt; gradually add to butter mixture, blending thoroughly. Add ¼ cup of the crushed candy canes and mix until well combined.

Roll dough into ¾-inch balls, then roll in remaining sugar (about ¼ cup) to coat. Place balls about 2 inches apart on greased and flour-dusted baking sheets. Flatten cookies with a fork, making a crisscross pattern with fork tines. Sprinkle each with about ½ teaspoon crushed candy canes.

Bake in a 325° oven for 18 to 20 minutes or until edges are lightly browned. Let cool on baking sheets for 2 to 3 minutes, then transfer to racks and let cool completely. Store airtight. Makes about 4 dozen.

Gingerbread Log Cabin *(Recipe on facing page)*

1 Start with a 6-inch log in back, two 2-inch logs in front. Top with 6-inch logs on sides, letting ends extend. Continue building, using spacers at inner edges of 2-inch logs.

2 Fourth layer uses 6-inch logs all around. Add 3 spacers across doorway; then top with 6-inch logs across front and back.

3 Using spacers and 3½ and 2-inch logs, build up gables on front and back of cabin. Place a spacer on top of each gable.

4 Ice and sugar roof pieces; ice top logs and spacers. Set roof in place, trimmed edges together.

Nürnberger Lebkuchen

(Pictured on pages 83 and 94)

In Nürnberg, Germany, Christmas baking begins in November with the preparation of *lebkuchen* — spicy, cakelike honey cookies that need to age for several weeks to become soft and chewy.

> 1 **cup honey**
> ¾ **cup firmly packed dark brown sugar**
> 1 **egg, lightly beaten**
> 1 **tablespoon lemon juice**
> 1 **teaspoon grated lemon peel**
> 2⅓ **cups all-purpose flour**
> 1 **teaspoon ground cinnamon**
> ½ **teaspoon** *each* **ground allspice, cloves, and nutmeg**
> ½ **teaspoon** *each* **salt and baking soda**
> ⅓ **cup** *each* **finely chopped candied citron and finely chopped almonds**
> **About 24 candied cherries, cut in half**
> 6 **to 8 ounces whole blanched almonds**
> **Glaze (recipe follows)**

Heat honey in a small pan over medium-high heat just until it begins to bubble. Remove from heat and let cool slightly. Stir in sugar, egg, lemon juice, and lemon peel; let cool to lukewarm.

In a large mixing bowl, stir together flour, cinnamon, allspice, cloves, nutmeg, salt, and baking soda. Add honey mixture, citron, and chopped almonds; stir until well blended (dough will be soft). Cover tightly with plastic wrap and refrigerate for at least 8 hours or for up to 2 days.

Work with a fourth of the dough at a time, keeping remaining dough refrigerated. On a heavily floured board, roll out dough with a floured rolling pin to a thickness of ⅜ inch. Cut dough with a 2½-inch round cookie cutter; place cookies 2 inches apart on baking sheets lined with lightly greased parchment paper.

Press a cherry half into center of each cookie; surround with 3 almonds arranged like flower petals. Bake in a 375° oven for 12 to 15 minutes or until golden brown. Meanwhile, prepare glaze. Remove cookies from oven and immediately brush glaze over tops with a pastry brush; transfer to racks and let cool. As soon as top glaze dries, turn cookies over and brush glaze over bottoms.

When cookies are completely cooled and dry, pack into airtight containers and store at room temperature for at least 2 weeks or for up to 3 months. If cookies get slightly hard, add a thin slice of apple to each container; cover tightly and store until cookies are moist again (about 1 day), then discard apple. Makes about 4 dozen.

Glaze. Stir together 1 cup **powdered sugar** and 5 tablespoons **rum** or water until very smooth.

Gingerbread Boys

(Pictured on page 94)

Full of personality, crisp gingerbread boys hang like holiday puppets on your Christmas tree.

> ½ **cup (¼ lb.) butter or margarine, softened**
> 1 **cup firmly packed brown sugar**
> 1½ **cups light molasses**
> ⅔ **cup water or apple juice**
> 6½ **cups all-purpose flour**
> 2 **teaspoons** *each* **baking soda and salt**
> 1 **teaspoon** *each* **ground cinnamon, ginger, cloves, and allspice**
> **Raisins**
> 1 **egg white, lightly beaten**
> **Purchased decorating icing (in tubes or aerosol cans)**

In large bowl of an electric mixer, beat butter and sugar until creamy. Add molasses and beat until blended, then mix in water. In another bowl, stir together flour, baking soda, salt, cinnamon, ginger, cloves, and allspice. Gradually add to butter mixture, blending to form a stiff dough. Cover tightly with plastic wrap and refrigerate for several hours or until next day.

On a floured board, roll out dough, a portion at a time, to a thickness of ³⁄₁₆ inch. Cut out with a 4 to 6-inch gingerbread boy cutter and, with cutter still in place, transfer cookie and cutter with a wide spatula to a lightly greased baking sheet. Lift off cutter and repeat. If desired, insert a short length of plastic drinking straw into each cookie near the top to make a hole for hanging; press straw all the way through to baking sheet.

Dip raisins in egg white and press them firmly into dough to make buttons (use about 3 per cookie). Move arms and legs to animate the figures.

Bake in a 350° oven for 10 to 15 minutes or until lightly browned. Transfer cookies to racks, remove straws (if used), and let cool completely. Draw faces on cooled cookies with icing. Tie ribbon or thread through holes for hanging, if desired. Store airtight. Makes about 4 dozen.

Speculaas

(Pictured on page 83)

Cookies are to the Netherlands as *Wienerbrød* is to Denmark and *Torten* are to Austria—a specialty of the country. As long ago as the 17th century, some Dutch bakers produced cookies exclusively. The very word "cookie" is our phonetic approximation of the Dutch *koekje* (little cake).

In Dutch homes, cookies are baked in profusion for *Sinterklaas avond* (the eve of St. Nicholas Day). Perhaps the best known of these holiday treats are crisp and spicy *speculaas*, traditionally shaped by pressing the dough into elaborately carved wooden molds. If you have a speculaas mold (they're sometimes sold in cookware shops), you'll be able to make cookies with old-fashioned embossed designs; if you don't, you can just roll out the dough and cut it with your favorite holiday cookie cutters.

> 2 cups all-purpose flour
> 2 teaspoons ground cinnamon
> ½ teaspoon *each* baking powder and ground nutmeg
> 1 teaspoon ground cloves
> ⅛ teaspoon salt
> ¼ cup ground blanched almonds
> 1 cup firmly packed brown sugar
> ¾ cup (¼ lb. plus 4 tablespoons) firm butter or margarine, cut into pieces
> 2 tablespoons milk

In a large bowl, stir together flour, cinnamon, baking powder, nutmeg, cloves, and salt. Blend in almonds and sugar until well combined. With a pastry blender or 2 knives, cut in butter until mixture resembles cornmeal; stir in milk. Work dough with your hands until you can form it into a smooth ball.

For molded cookies: Press dough firmly and evenly into a floured wooden speculaas mold; invert onto an ungreased baking sheet and release cookie by tapping back of mold (ease cookies out with the point of a knife, if necessary). Space cookies about 1 inch apart.

For rolled cookies: On a lightly floured board, roll out dough to a thickness of about ¼ inch. Cut out with 2 to 3-inch cookie cutters. Transfer to ungreased baking sheets, spacing cookies about 1 inch apart.

Bake in a 300° oven for 20 to 25 minutes or until lightly browned. Let cool briefly on baking sheets; transfer to racks and let cool completely. Store airtight. Makes about 4 dozen.

Anise Pretzels

(Pictured on page 94)

The attractive shape of these anise-flavored holiday cookies makes them a good choice for gifts, parties, or hanging on the tree. The anise flavor may remind you of *springerle*, an old-fashioned German cookie—and if you wish, you can shape the dough as you would for springerle, using the traditional carved rolling pin to produce little square cookies with embossed patterns.

> 1 cup (½ lb.) butter or margarine, softened
> ½ cup sugar
> 2 eggs
> 1½ teaspoons anise extract
> 3½ cups all-purpose flour
> 1 egg beaten with 1 tablespoon water (omit if shaping dough with a springerle rolling pin)
> 1 to 2 tablespoons anise seeds

In large bowl of an electric mixer, beat butter and sugar until creamy; beat in the 2 eggs, one at a time, beating until well combined after each addition. Beat in anise extract. Gradually add flour, blending thoroughly.

Divide dough in half. For pretzels, roll each half into a log 2 inches in diameter. For picture cookies, shape each half into a rectangular slab. Wrap tightly in plastic wrap and refrigerate until easy to handle (at least 1 hour).

For pretzels: Cut logs of dough into ⅜-inch-thick slices. Roll each slice into a rope about 14 inches long, then twist into a pretzel shape. Place on greased baking sheets, spacing at least 1 inch apart. Brush with egg-water mixture, then sprinkle lightly with anise seeds. Bake in a 325° oven for about 20 minutes or until light golden and firm to the touch. Transfer to racks and let cool. Store airtight. Makes about 2 dozen.

For picture cookies: On a lightly floured board, roll out dough, half at a time, to form a ¼-inch-thick rectangle slightly wider than your springerle rolling pin. Pressing down firmly, roll springerle rolling pin once over dough so that designs are sharply imprinted. With a sharp knife, cut pictures into squares, following lines made by springerle rolling pin.

Sprinkle each of 2 greased baking sheets with about 1 tablespoon anise seeds. Set cookies about 1 inch apart on seeds. Bake in a 325° oven for 15 to 18 minutes or until bottoms are golden and tops are firm to the touch but still white. Transfer to racks and let cool. Store airtight. Makes about 3½ dozen.

Dear, Santa Claus
I would like a dollhouse and a Kitten and a pony for Christmas.
Thank you.
Love, Alexandra

Index

Santa is sure to feel welcome when he sees the tree decorated with Anise Pretzels (page 93), Gingerbread Boys (page 92), and Stained-glass Cookies (page 88). A plate of Nürnberger Lebkuchen (page 92) and Fruitcake Cookie Cups (page 87)—with hot cocoa to sip alongside—might tempt him to stay until New Year's Day!

Metric Conversion Table

To change	To	Multiply by
ounces (oz.)	grams (g)	28
pounds (lbs.)	kilograms (kg)	0.45
teaspoons	milliliters (ml)	5
tablespoons	milliliters (ml)	15
fluid ounces (fl. oz.)	milliliters (ml)	30
cups	liters (l)	0.24
pints (pt.)	liters (l)	0.47
quarts (qt.)	liters (l)	0.95
gallons (gal.)	liters (l)	3.8
Fahrenheit temperature (°F)	Celsius temperature (°C)	⅝ after subtracting 32